TWELVE KEYS TO AN EFFECTIVE CHURCH
The Leaders' Guide

To honor the memory of
Gene St. Clair
wise, trusted, close friend
excellent leader
greatly missed and gently present

TWELVE KEYS
TO AN
EFFECTIVE CHURCH

The Leaders'
Guide

KENNON L. CALLAHAN

1817

Harper & Row, Publishers, San Francisco

New York, Grand Rapids, Philadelphia, St. Louis
London, Singapore, Sydney, Tokyo, Toronto

The National Institute for Church Planning and Consultation,
of which Kennon L. Callahan is the founder and senior consultant, can be addressed at 15775 Hillcrest #455, Dallas, TX
75248.

Designer: Rosalie Blazej

The Library of Congress has cataloged the main work as follows:
Callahan, Kennon L.
   Twelve keys to an effective church : strategic planning
for mission / Kennon L. Callahan. — 1st ed. — San Francisco : Harper & Row, c1983.
   xxxi, 127 p. ; 22 cm.
   ISBN 0-06-061295-9

   1. Church growth.   2. Missions.   3. Church manage-
ment. I. Title.
   BV652.25.C34 1983   254'.5 — dc19   83-47718
                                            AACR 2 MARC
   Library of Congress

91 HC 10 9 8

Contents

Introduction: Leaders and Long-range Planning

The purpose of planning is action, not planning. The purpose of planning is mission, not meetings. The purpose of effective long-range planning is accomplishments and achievements, not more activities and longer planning reports.

Many churches make the mistake of assuming that long-range planning should take a long time. Some churches have even had long-range planning committees that have been in existence for three years—and they have yet to develop a single long-range objective. They almost work out of the assumption that the longer they take, the better the plan. Not true. The more straightforward and streamlined the work of the long-range planning committee, the better the long-range plan.

The purpose of *Twelve Keys: The Leaders' Guide* is to help you help your church move toward action, accomplishment, and achievement, not more planning, more meetings, and longer reports. The *Leaders' Guide* is designed to provide you with the principles and resources to help your church decide its long-range plan in a timely, straightforward, streamlined way.

Twelve Keys: The Leaders' Guide is a direct companion book to *Twelve Keys to an Effective Church*, which has become the foundational, classic text in long-range planning for churches. Also related is *Twelve Keys: The Planning Workbook*, a book designed to help each local church discover, develop, and decide its effective long-range plan. Together these three works form a trilogy of planning resources for your church. Table 1 will help you to determine which of these books are recommended for use by each individual and group involved in long-range planning in your church.

You, the Grass Roots, and Key Leaders

Note that the title of this particular book is plural, not singular. It is the *Leaders' Guide*, not the *Leader's Guide*. It takes

Table 1.   Appropriate Use of the Twelve Keys Trilogy

	Twelve Keys to an Effective Church	Twelve Keys: The Leaders' Guide	Twelve Keys: The Planning Workbook
You, grass roots, key leaders	Study	Recommended	Use
Pastor, staff, steering committee	Study	Use	Use
Long-range planning committee	Study	Recommended	Use

a *team* of leaders to develop an effective long-range plan, and that team includes you, people from the grass roots of your congregation, key leaders, and your pastor and staff. Further, the team includes any resource leaders, long-range planning leaders, or consultants you invite to help your church in its long-range planning. The *Leaders' Guide* has not been written for a select few people. The principles and resources in it will be helpful to many people. Encourage a wide range of people—both grass roots and key leaders—to become familiar with it as well as with *Twelve Keys to an Effective Church.*

The *Leaders' Guide* is helpful in three important ways. First and most important, the resources of the book help you in the development of an effective long-range plan for your church. Second, the principles in the *Leaders' Guide* also apply to your work and business. Third, the insights you learn from the book are helpful in your everyday life—as you develop the sense of direction for your own life's pilgrimage.

When I wrote *Twelve Keys to an Effective Church* I did not envision the extraordinary impact the book would have throughout the church. Moreover, I did not anticipate all the ways in which the principles in *Twelve Keys to an Effective Church* would contribute to many people in their work and business and in their everyday lives. But again and again, as I have traveled throughout the country, countless people have spoken to me of the insights the book has brought them—in their church, in their work, and in their everyday life. Thus, as I have worked on the *Leaders' Guide,* I have kept these widespread applications fully in mind.

You should first study *Twelve Keys to an Effective Church.* Then encourage a representative group of people, both grass roots and key leaders, to study *Twelve Keys: The Leaders' Guide.* When you ask the grass roots and key leaders of your congregation to read both *Twelve Keys to an Effective Church* and *Twelve Keys: The Leaders' Guide,* share with them these three important ways they will be helped. The more people who are familiar with the content of both books, the stronger and more effective your long-range plan will be.

The Pastor, the Steering Committee, and the Long-range Planning Committee

The *Leaders' Guide* is especially helpful to the pastor and the staff of your church, and to the committees set up to organize, determine, and implement long-range planning. I generally recommend that two such committees be formed: the long-range planning steering committee and the long-range planning committee. The primary distinction between a long-range planning steering committee and a long-range planning committee is this: The *steering committee* consists of five to twelve persons who act as resources and lead the long-range planning committee and the congregation in the development of its effective long-range plan. The long-range *planning committee,* generally a much larger group, includes all people who participate in the four stages and six planning sessions. *Twelve Keys to an Effective Church* and *Twelve Keys: The Planning Workbook* will help the long-range planning committee to develop your long-range plan.

Resource Leaders, Planning Leaders, and Consultants

Frequently local churches invite a resource leader, a long-range planning leader, or a consultant to assist them in developing their long-range plan. It is important that each of these persons be familiar with the resources in *Twelve Keys to an Effective Church, Twelve Keys: The Planning Workbook,* and *Twelve Keys: The Leaders' Guide.*

A resource leader has an in-depth expertise and knowledge of the material and principles in *Twelve Keys to an Effective Church* and frequently leads a study of the twelve central characteristics of an effective church before the actual planning sessions. People from the grass roots and key leaders participate. Each member of the long-range planning steering committee is helped and coached by the resource leader to become knowledgeable as a "resident expert" in one or more of the twelve characteristics. The resource leader is familiar in depth with all twelve characteristics and helps the steering committee, as a whole, act as the resident expert team for the congregation.

A long-range planning leader primarily helps a local church by leading it through the four stages and six sessions of long-range planning. Thus a long-range planning leader should be thoroughly familiar with the *Planning Workbook* and the *Leaders' Guide*. To be sure, the long-range planning leader has an in-depth knowledge of the materials in *Twelve Keys to an Effective Church*. At the same time a long-range planning leader goes one step further—that is, the long-range planning leader provides leadership to the steering committee in helping the long-range planning committee and the congregation move through the four stages of long-range planning. Frequently this helps to advance the planning in a given local church.

It is important to note that leaders, pastors, and staff in local congregations will frequently become sufficiently familiar with the *Twelve Keys* materials and principles that they emerge as resource leaders and long-range planning leaders with their own church and with other churches in the area. The more persons who can serve as resource leaders and long-range planning leaders, the stronger the long-range planning in local congregations.

A consultant has an in-depth expertise and knowledge of the resources, principles, and materials in all three works. A consultant may first serve as a resource leader with several congregations, leading them in a study of *Twelve Keys to an Effective Church*. Then the consultant may serve as a long-range planning leader with several local churches, leading them in the use of *Twelve Keys: The Planning Workbook* and sharing with them the resources in *Twelve Keys: The Leaders' Guide*. Having served as resource leader and long-range planning leader with a number of congregations, the person is likely to emerge as a consultant. We need to increase the number of competent consultants available to local churches.

The consultant has the expertise of the resource leader and the competencies of the long-range planning leader and does one thing more—the consultant shares his or her best wisdom, judgment, vision, common sense, and prayer regarding the best way forward for a given congregation. The resource leader can share the content of *Twelve Keys* but stops short of sharing his or her best wisdom and judgment. The long-range planning leader can share the four stages of effective long-range planning in the *Planning Workbook* and the resources in the *Leaders' Guide* but stops short of answering the question, What do you think? The consultant is the one of the three who answers the question, What is your best judgment? The consultant shares his or her best mutual wisdom and judgment, vision and common sense and does so in a prayerful, compassionate, coaching way.

All three—the resource leader, the long-range planning leader, and the consultant—are helpful. Sometimes a person will serve as resource leader with one church, planning leader with another church, and consultant with yet a third church. You may want to consider serving other local congregations in one or more of these ways.

The Three-Part Approach

The *Leaders' Guide* is divided into three parts. Each part makes a distinctive contribution and it will be beneficial for you to become thoroughly familiar with the material in each part. As a whole the *Leaders' Guide* shares the foundational principles that are valuable for you to know as you help your church develop an effective long-range plan.

Part 1 contains the resources that help you develop your long-range plan. Part 2 includes the resources that help you launch, move forward, and accomplish your long-range plan. The resources in part 3 help both as you develop your plan and as you move forward to achieve it.

Part 1 focuses on the qualitative resources, the invitational perspective, and the major considerations important to developing an effective long-range plan. Part 1 includes these resources:

- An outline of the four stages of long-range planning and the six planning sessions that I recommend, with useful suggestions for the six planning sessions

- A discussion of the nature of timelines, the criteria for key objectives, and the focus of long-range planning
- A discussion of the major qualitative resources for effective long-range planning
- A discussion of the four invitational questions, which give direction to your planning
- Suggestions as to what to listen for and what to look for as you plan
- A discussion of nine principles to maximize participation in the development of your long-range plan

Part 2 focuses on the seven qualities found to be present in groups that have a strong record of action, implementation, and momentum. The presence of these qualities helps a local church to move into action that implements their plans and develops momentum further. As leaders seeking to accomplish an effective long-range plan for your church, you need to think through which of these qualities are currently present in your congregation and which of these qualities can be nurtured forward as your congregation moves toward its long-range future. Whenever these qualities are not fully present, that local church tends to have a much weaker track record of action, implementation, and momentum. By way of an overview these seven qualities are listed here:

1. An effective long-range plan
2. An excellent match between leaders and key objectives
3. An excellent match in terms of the motivational resources present among key leaders, the pastor, and the grass roots of the congregation
4. Leadership development that focuses on the "middle third," the middle range of competence
5. Recognition of the value of excellent mistakes
6. Recognition that some key objectives are worth not doing
7. A practice of prayer that focuses on the qualities of vision and hope

Part 3 focuses on the four dynamics operative in local churches. These four dynamics are present in every group of people, and they are present in your own life's pilgrimage as well. The four dynamics are memory, change, conflict, and hope. It is precisely these four dynamics, with their distinctive configuration in a given local church, that have major impact on any present moment or, indeed, on any future moment in the life of that church. An understanding of these four dynamics will be most helpful to you as leaders as you develop an effective long-range plan for your church.

One Possible Procedure

The following steps constitute one possible procedure for developing an effective long-range plan for your church's future. Use your best creativity to adapt and construct this procedure into the one that will be most helpful for your church.

Step 1. Study *Twelve Keys to an Effective Church*. The more people who are familiar with the twelve central characteristics of an effective church, the stronger and more accurate the long-range plan. Involve as many grass roots people and key leaders as possible. It is vital that each person on the long-range planning committee participate. Be sure the study is thorough and well done. Invite members of the steering committee or a resource leader to lead the study. Be sure the study is done briefly, over a one- to three-month period. There is an exception to this suggested timing. In many churches the board, session, or council has successfully studied one or two of the central characteristics in their regular monthly meetings over a six- to twelve-month period. These churches feel strongly that this plan of study has been immensely helpful to them. Think through the study plan that will work best for your church.

Step 2. Study *Twelve Keys: The Leaders' Guide*. The grass roots, key leaders, and long-range planning committee of the congregation should concentrate primarily on a study of *Twelve Keys to an Effective Church*. At the same time, or certainly before the planning sessions are held, it is valuable for the steering committee, the pastor, and the staff to study the *Leaders' Guide*. Frequently each person reads the book individually. Then the steering committee, the pastor, and staff may have three planned discussions—one each for part 1, part 2, and part 3. Three persons on the steering committee might each share leadership for one of these three discussions. Or if a planning leader has been invited to work with the steering committee, that person might lead these discussions. These three discussions would focus on the ways the resources in each part will be used by the steering committee as it leads the long-range planning committee and the congregation in developing its long-range plan.

Step 3. Develop your long-range plan by using *Twelve Keys: The Planning Workbook*. In a real sense there are two vital preparatory steps: One preparatory step for the long-range planning committee and congregation, namely, the study of *Twelve Keys to an Effective Church;* and one preparatory step for the steering committee, pastor, and staff, namely, the study of the *Leaders' Guide*. Then the steering committee leads the long-range planning committee through the four stages of effective long-range planning. These four stages are best accomplished in no more than six planning sessions, using *Twelve Keys: The Planning Workbook*. Each person on the long-range planning committee has his or her copy of the *Planning Workbook*. Each person selects his or her planning team partner and each planning team works through the four stages to achieve an effective long-range plan for your church.

Step 4. Study *Twelve Keys: The Leaders' Guide* again. Once you have established and are moving toward the accomplishment of your long-range plan, it is valuable for one or more persons on the steering committee to lead a study of the *Leaders' Guide*, particularly part 2. Mostly the steering committee will have used the materials in part 1 and part 3 to inform the development of the long-range plan in step 3. It is especially valuable, after your church has been working on its long-range plan for a time, to lead the board, session, or council in a study of part 2 and of the seven qualities that contribute to a strong track record of action, implementation, and momentum in local churches. This study might best be done in the monthly board meetings at some point during the first six months of the long-range plan. This step is particularly helpful in the *early* stages of your plan.

Part One
RESOURCES FOR
LONG-RANGE PLANNING

1. The Four Stages and Six Sessions

The *Planning Workbook* is organized so that your church can move through the four stages of effective long-range planning in six sessions. In many churches stages 1 and 2 are held in on-site planning discussions at the church, and stages 3 and 4 are then the focal points of a weekend planning retreat. In some churches these four stages are shared on consecutive Wednesday evenings, as a part of the Wednesday evening family night program. In many churches these four stages are shared on Sunday mornings during church school. In others they are shared on Sunday evenings as part of the special Sunday evening programing. Sometimes planning discussions are held once every two weeks over a three-month period. The variety is virtually endless.

Develop the planning schedule that works best for you and your church. But keep in mind that my experience indicates these four stages—decisive in shaping the long-range future for your church—are best accomplished in six concentrated planning sessions. The first three stages generally take one session apiece, and then stage 4 is the focus for the three final sessions.

For the benefit of your preparation and leadership of these six planning sessions, the following detailed outline is helpful:

An Outline for Effective Long-range Planning

Session 1: Introduction to the four stages and overview
    Stage 1. Develop a realistic assessment of your church's present standing and stature
    Introduction to Stage 2

Session 2: Stage 2. Choose the primary direction for your future
    Phase 1. Determine where you are now

Phase 2. Discover how far you can go
Phase 3. Decide how far you want to go
Introduction to Stage 3

Session 3: Stage 3. Study your strengths in relation to the twelve central characteristics of an effective church
Phase 1. Prepare a preliminary analysis
Phase 2. Analyze and diagnose the relational characteristics of your church
Phase 3. Analyze and diagnose the functional characteristics of your church
Introduction to Stage 4

Session 4: Stage 4. Select the central characteristics, key objectives, and timelines that will advance your church's future
Phase 1. Share and analyze your planning team ratings of the twelve central characteristics
Phase 2. Select the strengths you would like to expand and add
Introduction to Phases 3 and 4

Session 5: Stage 4, continued
Phase 3. Meet with other planning teams to determine which characteristics to expand and add
Phase 4. Construct a timeline for the coming three to five years
Introduction to Phase 5

Session 6: Stage 4, continued
Phase 5. Determine your key objectives for expanding and adding characteristics

The following discussion of each session will help you keep your church focused and on track in its long-range planning process.

Session One

Stage 1. Develop a realistic assessment of your church's present standing and stature

During the first session it is important to help your local church develop a realistic assessment of its present standing and stature, strength and vitality, size and consequence. I frequently refer to the formula P→B→D. Perception yields Behavior and Behavior yields Destiny. Regrettably many churches tend to have unrealistically limited perceptions of themselves. They compare themselves with First Baptist or University Presbyterian and say, "We're not as big as they are," and they tend to underestimate themselves.

Churches tend to grow toward the size of the mission they share in the community. This is one of the reasons we have so many stable and declining and dying churches across the country. Medium-sized churches that perceive themselves as small churches eventually grow downward to that small size. A church that perceives itself as a small church makes small plans. Its key objectives are kept in line with small church standards. And consequently, it shares a small-sized mission in the community. Because of that perception of being small it shares a small-sized mission in the community.

We also have many large churches that think of themselves as medium-sized churches, and they tend to share a mission in the community commensurate with a medium-sized church. Soon they have grown downward to the size of that medium-sized mission. There is a direct correlation between a church's perception of itself and the size of the mission it shares in its community. And churches will grow—forward or downward—to the size of the mission they share in the community. So it is important in long-range planning for a church to first develop a realistic and accurate perception of itself.

Regrettably denominations often tend to refer to only two categories of churches; they tend to divide them into small churches and large churches. It is inaccurate, though, to work with only these two categories of churches. If we are going to refer to churches by size at all, let's think of small, medium, and large churches. And let's use more than the category of membership to define the strength and vitality of a church. It is more accurate to use four categories: average worship attendance, average church school attendance, church school enrollment, and membership. The greater weight should be placed on the categories of average worship attendance and average church school attendance, since those two are categories of participation and are likely to be stronger indicators of the genuine standing and stature, strength and vitality, and size and consequence of a local church.

There is no merit in being bigger—to be bigger is to be bigger, not necessarily better. Some churches romanticize bigness; and as a counter to that other churches romanticize smallness. The reality is that the Lord invites a church to share a mission commensurate with its present strength and vitality. When a small-sized church shares a small-sized mission, the Lord says, "Well done!" When a medium-sized church shares a medium-sized mission, the Lord says, "Well done!" And when a large-sized church shares a large-sized mission, the Lord says, "Well done!" The first session helps a church develop a realistic assessment so that its behavior in mission can be commensurate with its real standing and stature, size and consequence, and strength and vitality.

Session Two

Stage 2. Choose the primary direction for your future

In the second session it is important to help your local church successfully accomplish stage 2 in the *Planning Workbook*. In stage 2 you are invited to determine the following: where you are now, how far you can go, and how far you want to go.

Phase 1 Determine where you are now

During this first phase in helping your church choose the primary direction for its future, you help your church discover where you are now in the total number of people your church serves. Most local churches serve more people than they think they do. While people often think of their church primarily in terms of how many members—300, 500, 700 members—it has, average worship attendance, average church school attendance, church school enrollment, and church membership, taken together, are better indicators than membership alone. Now let's go a step further—the *best* way to think of your church is in terms of the *total number of people served*, some of whom are members, some of whom are constituents, and some of whom are persons served in mission.

I was once helping a church and I asked the people there how many members they had, and they indicated that they had 500 members. Then I asked, "How many constituents do you have?" They had no idea; they thought a constituent was some sort of a disease. A *constituent* is a nonmember who participates two to four times in a six-month period in some activity in your church. All children who are not yet members are constituents. All persons, of whatever age, who are nonmembers and who participate two to four times in a six-month period in some activity related to your church are constituents. The people I explained this to could think of 450 constituents who were a part of the life and work of their church.

Next I asked these people, "How many people does your church serve in mission in a year's time?" A *person served in mission* is a nonmember or a nonconstituent in the local community who is directly helped with a specific human hurt and that helping is directly linked to your church. The people I was talking to could think of approximately 300 persons in the local community whom their church had helped in one way or another during the previous year.

Then I asked these people, "What is the total number of people your church serves?" And they said, "Well, we have 500 members." They hadn't *yet* gotten the message. The total number of people served by that church was 1,250 persons.

Some churches focus on the question, "How many staff members should we have in relation to our membership?" That is an interesting question, but not very helpful. A better focus would be, "How many staff members should we have in relation to the total persons served in this church (some of whom are members, some of whom are constituents, and some of whom are persons served in mission)?" Most churches that have a high concern for people, service, and quality are staffing themselves with key leaders, volunteers, and paid staff in relation to the total number of people served. In the previous example the total number of people served would be 1,250 persons. To use the medical term, that is the total patient load. To use the missional term, that is the total number of people served in mission by this church in a given year.

Phase 2 Discover how far you can go

In the second phase you help your church discover how far you can go in light of your maximum mission potential. Most churches have a stronger maximum mission potential than they are aware of. Many are still acting as though it were the churched culture of the 1950s. Regrettably many churches have a mission statement that sounds like the nursery rhyme about Little Bo Peep: "leave them alone and they'll come home . . ." These churches live under the myth that when young couples have their first baby they will be back at church. This does sometimes happen—just enough times in a decade to make the myth believable, when in fact it is a myth.

Churches also perpetuate the myth that newcomers—if they want a church—"know where we are and will find us." There are just enough newcomers who do come into a church to visit during a decade to make them believe this, when in fact it is a myth. This is one of the richest mission fields on this planet. And it is most important that in this phase your church discovers its maximum mission potential.

Phase 3 Decide how far you want to go

The object of the third phase is to decide how far you want to go—that is, to think through your objective as to the number of new people you will serve in mission in each year of your long-range plan—the first year, the second year, the third year, and so on.

You now know the maximum mission potential of your church. How many new people can you realistically hope to serve in your community each year? People you are not now serving, people you will seek out and find, people you can help in relation to specific human hurts and hopes.

Note that the very step of selecting a missional objective is a new venture for many congregations. The setting of a missional objective invites your church to be self-giving rather than self-seeking and self-serving. Since the churched culture days of the 1950s, churches have set objectives year after year with respect to the number of new members they plan to reach, the increase in worship attendance they hope to achieve, and the number of church school enrollments they hope to accomplish. But rarely have local churches thought through a specific missional objective as to the number of new people whom they look forward to reaching in mission during the coming year. Simply setting this missional objective honors the fact that it is a new day—that we are in fact on a mission field in our time.

I'm not proposing that the congregation try to serve its full maximum mission potential in the first year of its long-range plan. Depending on the size of the maximum mission potential available to a given church, it would be a reasonable objective for a church to seek to serve 15 to 20 percent of that total maximum mission potential in the first year of an effective long-range plan.

Session Three

Stage 3. Study your strengths in relation to the twelve characteristics of an effective church

In the third session the participants cover stage 3 in the *Planning Workbook* and study and evaluate the relational and functional characteristics of successful, effective churches in mission. There are three phases to this stage:

Phase 1. Prepare a preliminary analysis
Phase 2. Analyze and diagnose the relational characteristics of your church
Phase 3. Analyze and diagnose the functional characteristics of your church

It is most helpful for the participants to be familiar with the chapters in *Twelve Keys to an Effective Church* as they share their analysis and diagnosis of their church in relation to each of the twelve central characteristics. The more accurate the diagnosis and analysis, the more creative and constructive will be the long-range plan that emerges from these six sessions.

Session Four

Stage 4. Select the central characteristics, key objectives, and timelines that will advance your church's future

In the fourth session it is important to help participants complete phases 1 and 2 of stage 4 in the *Planning Workbook*. As leaders you will find this a most creative part of the planning to facilitate and coordinate.

Phase 1 Share and analyze your planning team ratings for the twelve central characteristics

The *Planning Workbook* suggests that you have your long-range planning committee divide into two-person planning teams to do much of the previous analysis. You should now have the planning teams come together to share and record all of their ratings of the twelve central characteristics. All of the participants have an opportunity to get some feedback regarding the wisdom and judgment of all the planning teams. It is important that this phase not be hurried but be thoughtfully shared as the planning team ratings are recorded in both the *Planning Workbook* and on an overhead transparency or a chalkboard for all to share with one another.

Phase 2 Select the strengths you would like to expand and add

After everyone has had the chance to share his or her best diagnosis and analysis of the ratings, it becomes important for each planning team to determine thoughtfully and creatively which of its current strengths (characteristics with ratings of 8, 9 or 10) it makes sense to expand. Likewise each planning team then thinks through which characteristics (rated 1 through 7) are important to add as strengths in order to be more effective in mission as a church.

When you develop a long-range plan the most strategic decisions involve choosing which central characteristics to expand and which central characteristics to add. Pick a few. Do this well. It is important that each planning team be given ample opportunity to think through its best recommendations for the future of the church.

Decisive to the development of an effective long-range plan is the selection of those central characteristics that it makes best sense for your church to expand and add. No set of decisions is more important than this. Local churches frequently make one of two mistakes: (1) they include too many "expands" and "adds" in their long-range plan, or (2) they move too quickly to key objectives before deciding the central characteristics that are their best major priorities as "expands" and "adds."

The art is to expand and add those specific central characteristics that not only build on the current strengths of your church but also match well with the strengths and competencies of the leadership of your church and the distinctive community

The Twelve Central Characteristics

Relational Characteristics	Functional Characteristics
1. Specific, Concrete Missional Objectives 1 ②　3　4　5　6　7　8　9　10	7. Several Competent Programs and Activities 1　2　3　4　5 ⑥ 7　8　9　10
2. Pastoral/Lay Visitation in Community 1　2　3 ④ 5　6　7　8　9　10	8. <u>Open Accessibility</u> 1　2　3　4　5　6　7 ⑧ 9　10
3. <u>Corporate, Dynamic Worship</u> 1　2　3　4　5　6　7 ⑧ 9　10	9. <u>High Visibility</u> 1　2　3　4　5　6　7 ⑧ 9　10
4. Significant Relational Groups 1　2　3　4　5 ⑥ 7　8　9　10	10. Adequate Parking, Land and Landscaping 1　2 ③ 4　5　6　7　8　9　10
5. <u>Strong Leadership Resources</u> 1　2　3　4　5　6　7 ⑧ 9　10	11. Adequate Space and Facilities 1　2　3　4　5　6 ⑦ 8　9　10
6. <u>Solid, Participatory Decision Making</u> 1　2　3　4　5　6　7　8 ⑨ 10	12. Solid Financial Resources 1　2　3　4　5 ⑥ 7　8　9　10

Figure 1. A Sample Rating of the Central Characteristics

your church seeks to serve. Thus, while it is possible that three churches might have the same ratings for all twelve central characteristics, they would still develop three distinctive long-range plans. This is illustrated in figures 1 to 4.

Figure 1 presents a set of ratings shared by three different churches. In this figure a rating has been circled for each characteristic. Those characteristics with ratings of 8, 9, or 10 have been underlined once to indicate they are current strengths.

Figures 2, 3, and 4 show that, based on its available leadership resources and its distinctive community, each church has chosen a unique set of central characteristics to expand and add. In these figures current strengths to be expanded have been underlined a second time, and characteristics to be added as new strengths in the future have been circled.

Independently and individually the leaders and grass roots of each of these churches have done a thoughtful analysis and diagnosis of their ratings in relation to the twelve central characteristics of an effective church in stages 1 to 3. Then in stage 4, guided by wisdom, judgment, vision, common sense, and prayer, they have decided which central characteristics they will expand and which they want to add as future strengths in each church.

The Twelve Central Characteristics

Relational Characteristics	*Functional Characteristics*
1. Specific, Concrete Missional Objectives 1 (2) 3 4 5 6 7 8 9 10	7. Several Competent Programs and Activities 1 2 3 4 5 (6) 7 8 9 10
2. Pastoral/Lay Visitation in Community 1 2 3 (4) 5 6 7 8 9 10	8. Open Accessibility 1 2 3 4 5 6 7 (8) 9 10
3. Corporate, Dynamic Worship 1 2 3 4 5 6 7 (8) 9 10	9. High Visibility 1 2 3 4 5 6 7 (8) 9 10
4. Significant Relational Groups 1 2 3 4 5 (6) 7 8 9 10	10. Adequate Parking, Land and Landscaping 1 2 (3) 4 5 6 7 8 9 10
5. Strong Leadership Resources 1 2 3 4 5 6 7 (8) 9 10	11. Adequate Space and Facilities 1 2 3 4 5 6 (7) 8 9 10
6. Solid, Participatory Decision Making 1 2 3 4 5 6 7 8 (9) 10	12. Solid Financial Resources 1 2 3 4 5 (6) 7 8 9 10

Figure 2. Characteristics to Be Expanded or Added by Church A

The Twelve Central Characteristics

Relational Characteristics	*Functional Characteristics*
1. Specific, Concrete Missional Objectives 1 (2) 3 4 5 6 7 8 9 10	7. Several Competent Programs and Activities 1 2 3 4 5 (6) 7 8 9 10
2. Pastoral/Lay Visitation in Community 1 2 3 (4) 5 6 7 8 9 10	8. Open Accessibility 1 2 3 4 5 6 7 (8) 9 10
3. Corporate, Dynamic Worship 1 2 3 4 5 6 7 (8) 9 10	9. High Visibility 1 2 3 4 5 6 7 (8) 9 10
4. Significant Relational Groups 1 2 3 4 5 (6) 7 8 9 10	10. Adequate Parking, Land and Landscaping 1 2 (3) 4 5 6 7 8 9 10
5. Strong Leadership Resources 1 2 3 4 5 6 7 (8) 9 10	11. Adequate Space and Facilities 1 2 3 4 5 6 (7) 8 9 10
6. Solid, Participatory Decision Making 1 2 3 4 5 6 7 8 (9) 10	12. Solid Financial Resources 1 2 3 4 5 (6) 7 8 9 10

Figure 3. Characteristics to be Expanded or Added by Church B

The Twelve Central Characteristics

Relational Characteristics	Functional Characteristics
1. Specific, Concrete Missional Objectives 1 ②3 4 5 6 7 8 9 10	7. Several Competent Programs and Activities 1 2 3 4 5 ⑥7 8 9 10
2. Pastoral/Lay Visitation in Community 1 2 3 ④5 6 7 8 9 10	8. Open Accessibility 1 2 3 4 5 6 7 ⑧9 10
3. Corporate, Dynamic Worship 1 2 3 4 5 6 7 ⑧9 10	9. High Visibility 1 2 3 4 5 6 7 ⑧9 10
4. Significant Relational Groups 1 2 3 4 5 ⑥7 8 9 10	10. Adequate Parking, Land and Landscaping 1 2 ③4 5 6 7 8 9 10
5. Strong Leadership Resources 1 2 3 4 5 6 7 ⑧9 10	11. Adequate Space and Facilities 1 2 3 4 5 6 ⑦8 9 10
6. Solid, Participatory Decision Making 1 2 3 4 5 6 7 8 ⑨10	12. Solid Financial Resources 1 2 3 4 5 ⑥7 8 9 10

Figure 4. Characteristics to be Expanded or Added by Church C

Church A (see fig. 2) has decided that the best way forward, given its leadership resources and its specific community, is to expand corporate, dynamic worship and strong leadership resources. Hence, the planning team has double underlined these two characteristics. And they have decided to focus on adding specific, concrete missional objectives, pastoral and lay visitation in the community, several competent programs and activities, and adequate parking, land, and landscaping. They have circled these four characteristics that they plan to add as new strengths.

Church B (see fig. 3) has decided the best way forward is to expand the central characteristics of strong leadership resources and open accessibility and to add the central characteristics of specific, concrete missional objectives, significant relational groups, several competent programs and activities, and adequate space and facilities.

Church C (see fig. 4) has decided the best way forward is to expand the central characteristics of corporate, dynamic worship and high visibility and to add the central characteristics of pastoral and lay visitation in the community, significant relational groups, adequate parking, land, and landscaping, and solid financial resources.

Your planning group's best wisdom, judgment, vision, common sense, and prayer is needed to think through which is the best way forward for your distinctive church. As a key leader you can help your church discover those central characteristics that match best with your church's current strengths, with the gifts and competencies of your leadership team, and with the distinctive community your church seeks to serve.

The best plan does not necessarily have the longest list of objectives. The best plan lists those few key objectives related to expanding current strengths and adding new foundational strengths among the central characteristics of an effective church. Thus it makes good sense for each planning team to be given ample opportunity to think through these strategic decisions constructively and creatively.

Session Five

Stage 4, continued. Select the central characteristics, key objectives, and timelines that will advance your church's future

Phase 3 Meet with the other planning teams to determine which characteristics to expand and add

In Phase 3 the planning teams share with the group those central characteristics they are recommending as expands and adds for the church's future. Briefly sharing the distinctive recommendations of each planning team with the entire group frequently increases the spirit of creativity and momentum. Once all of the planning teams have had the opportunity to share their best thinking, then it is important for each person in the group—the key leaders and each planning team—to identify those central characteristics that have had the strongest consensus for expansion and those central characteristics that have had the strongest consensus for addition as new strengths.

Phase 4 Construct a timeline for the coming three to five years

Given the accomplishment of phase 3, the total planning group should have the opportunity to construct a timeline of solid work flow related to these expands and adds. In constructing a timeline your group should refer to the planning principles in "Conclusion: Principles and Priorities in Strategic Long-range Planning" in *Twelve Keys to an Effective Church*.

Once this has been achieved each planning team should identify the two to four key issues important to the church's future in light of the central characteristics the group as a whole thinks should be expanded and added. Having identified those two to four key issues, each planning team should have some time before the next session to consider the relationship of those two to four key issues to both work-flow timelines and the key objectives that will best accomplish an effective long-range plan.

Session Six

Stage 4, continued. Select the central characteristics, key objectives, and timelines that will advance your church's future

Phase 5 Determine your key objectives for expanding and adding characteristics

In the fifth session the group had the opportunity to chart a timeline to show how they would best lay out the work flow. There is a logical order in which they will want to expand and add specific central characteristics during the coming three to five years (or whatever time horizon the group has chosen). (See chapter 2 for more details on timelines.) Now each planning team identifies the key objectives that match best with each central characteristic to be expanded or added and determines the appropriate timelines for each key objective.

To *expand* a current strength you determine the two to four key objectives that will best advance that foundational strength toward a rating of 10 from its current rating of 8 or 9. Encourage each planning team to focus on thinking of only the two to four strongest objectives. You want to find the "twenty percenters"— those objectives that use 20 percent of your effort to yield 80 percent of your results. It is not helpful for a planning team to come up with ten, twelve, or fifteen objectives to expand a central characteristic. That only adds confusion to the planning process, and it likely introduces "eighty percenters" into the planning discussion. The most constructive and creative planning discussions are those in which the group makes a covenant to focus on only those key objectives that will be twenty percenters.

To *add* a new strength a planning team is encouraged to identify no more than four to six key objectives. Should a team tend to come up with long lists of objectives, invite them to focus on the four to six that they think will best add that central characteristic. It takes no more than four to six key objectives to establish a new central characteristic. Look for the four to six objectives that match best with this church and the community it seeks to serve as it puts in place that specific central characteristic.

Once each team has developed its own list of key objectives for expanding and adding each of the selected central characteristics, share those key objectives with the group. This should be done so that the group as a whole has the opportunity to select the best of the key objectives for each "expand" and the best of the key objectives for each "add."

Planning teams will want to note in their *Planning Workbook* the expands and adds and the best of the key objectives as they are selected. This is not to suggest that all of the various objectives from all of the other planning teams be recorded in the workbook. Rather, it is to suggest that those few excellent key objectives that the group feels will best advance forward the mission of the church be recorded. At the end of session 6 participants leave with a virtual summary of the church's long-range plan in their own *Planning Workbook*.

At the end of the sixth session the long-range plan is beginning to take shape. It may be helpful for the long-range planning steering committee to take the best of the discussion and to summarize the central characteristics and key objectives in the streamlined long-range planning document that can be circulated widely throughout the congregation.

2. Timelines, Objectives, and Long-range Planning

As key leaders in helping your local church to develop an effective long-range plan, you should help participants to understand the distinctive character of timelines and objectives and the nature of long-range planning.

Timelines

When you set specific timelines keep in mind the foundational principles for the development of timelines, discussed in some depth in *Twelve Keys to an Effective Church*. They are briefly mentioned here.

1. Develop confidence and competence. Focus on those key objectives that nurture the confidence and competence of the congregation. It is easier to expand a present strength than it is to add a new foundational strength. The congregation is more likely to tackle tough, hard problems when its confidence and competence have been developed. It is more likely to become tense and tight and to resist tackling tough problems when members feel they have been set up to fail in any aspect of the long-range plan. The art is to grow forward the confidence and competence of the congregation in its missional outreach in the community.

Many churches make the mistake of loading the first year of their long-range plan with more than they can accomplish in that year. Then they tend to be vague about the middle years of their plan and "hope to have everything accomplished by the last year." It is most important that there be a workable set of timelines demonstrating a reasonable work flow that the leaders and grass roots of the congregation can substantially achieve and accomplish.

2. Expand first those strengths that are easiest to expand. When you develop the first year of your long-range plan, if you

have a choice between expanding a current strength or adding a new one, the better choice is to expand a current strength. In the first year you must set up your church to succeed, not fail. Remember this principle: Build on your strengths—do better what you do best. Successfully expanding a current strength puts you in a stronger position to add new foundational strengths in the future.

3. Develop a natural rhythm. Select that combination of expands and adds and related key objectives that will develop a natural rhythm of momentum and a natural dynamic for your church. The sequential character of specific central characteristics is unique for each church.

4. Develop complementary priorities. Develop timelines that coordinate complementary priorities in the same years. They mutually reinforce one another.

One church announced that it had two key objectives for the coming year: to reach twenty new unchurched young couples with small children, and to build the choir's communitywide reputation for excellence by singing only classical music during the service of worship. Those were two excellent objectives. But they were not complementary priorities for that same year. Radio marketing surveys in that area indicated that young couples tended to listen to two kinds of music: soft rock FM and country-western. To coordinate the two objectives the music program planners could increase the choir's reputation by preparing well and singing Mozart's *Requiem* at Easter, and they could keep to the middle-of-the-road anthems during the Sunday services. They might initiate child care during choir rehearsals in order to attract some of the new young couples to the choir. Think through your timelines so that complementary priorities can mutually reinforce one another during each year of your long-range plan.

Objectives

Here are six important guidelines to follow in developing objectives for expanding or adding specific central characteristics.

1. Write down your objectives. There are two values to written objectives. First, distance. When an objective is written down on paper each member of a planning team can gain sufficient distance on it so that he or she can creatively evaluate

whether or not this will help the church be in mission. Second, covenant. When you have decided together on those written key objectives that will expand and add specific central characteristics, you have made a covenant with each other to head in that common direction. The value of each planning team writing its own key objectives in the planning workbook and then recording the key objectives on which the group decides is that each person leaves the last planning session with his or her own copy of the long-range plan that all agreed to achieve.

2. Be sure there is a sense of ownership. It is most important that the people who will work on accomplishing and achieving a specific key objective have a very strong sense of "ownership." It needs to be *their* objective, not something thrust on them by an outsider. The value of including as many people as possible in the long-range planning sessions is that the more people included, the more people who have ownership. It is their long-range plan. They have chosen the key objectives related to each central characteristic they want to achieve.

3. Make your objectives specific and measurable. An excellent key objective is sufficiently specific and measurable that one will know when that objective has been accomplished. For example, "Add fifteen new parking spaces on the west side of the church so we will have a total of seventy-five spaces there by October 1."

State the objective in such a way that whenever members of the church evaluate progress they can check it off as one they've accomplished. What few key objectives would you like to be celebrating two years from today? State them specifically and measurably.

Any objective that includes the word *more* is not an objective. Sometimes churches develop statements such as "we need more members," "we need more people in the choir," or "we need to reach more youth." The word *more* is a setup for failure. *More* is always one more over the horizon—you can never accomplish *more*. *More* is a never-ending horizon of failure. The same is true of *better*. How do you know if you have succeeded if you still need more or better?

4. Set realistic time horizons. An excellent key objective includes intermediary definite time horizons that build toward the desired end result. For example, while a church could have a key objective to increase the choir from twenty to thirty persons

in eighteen months, it would be more helpful to have realistic intermediary timetables, such as increasing the choir from twenty to twenty-three persons in six months; from twenty-three to twenty-six in the next six months; and from twenty-six to thirty persons by the end of the eighteen months. Steady, progressive growth is more likely to be achieved with those kinds of realistic time horizons than with a general objective to grow from twenty to thirty in eighteen months.

5. Make your objectives concrete and achievable. An excellent objective stretches the group members just enough that they grow forward and develop their strengths. But it is not a grandiose, glittering generality.

The mistake many churches make is that they set unrealistic and unachievable objectives. Some people have a theological perspective that has a built-in compulsiveness toward perfectionism, and when they set objectives with a group others may procrastinate and hang back from working. Compulsive, perfectionistic persons tend to set objectives that are too high and will never realistically be achieved. And since the others in the group innately sense that the objective has set them up to fail, they postpone action because they are seeking to postpone failure. Whenever you see that a group or a person is not mobilizing to accomplish an objective, one of the first things to look at is whether that objective is concrete and achievable.

6. Make your objectives complementary. Whenever you construct two or four key objectives to expand a current strength, be sure that they complement, supplement, and mutually reinforce one another. If they are divergent, if they head in different directions, look for a stronger match of objectives.

The Nature of Long-range Planning

In considering the nature of long-range planning compare these three logical options: (1) something will work, (2) nothing will work, and (3) everything will work. It is not realistic to believe that everything will work. Of the three options the third can immediately be disregarded. You should not work out of the conviction that everything will work. It is even more important that you not work out of the conviction that nothing will work.

You, your church's other key leaders, its pastor, grass roots, and long-range planning steering committee will develop an excellent long-range plan, pooling your best mutual wisdom, judgment, vision, common sense, and prayer. You will focus only on twenty percenters that deliver 80 percent of the results. You will give your most creative and constructive effort to developing an effective long-range plan. And you will do so out of the conviction that something will work.

You must not expect that everything will work. Frankly, not everything needs to work. A sufficient number of twenty percenter key objectives, working well, will grow forward the momentum and dynamic of a given church. The art is to think through in wholistic, integrative, dynamic ways those central characteristics to expand and those central characteristics to add in a way that creatively and constructively advances the whole. And to do so with the conviction that something will work.

I have served as consultant with churches that have had thirty-two losing years. I have served as consultant with churches that, in fact, border on the brink of the abyss, teetering on the edge, ready to fall. Many of those churches have come to believe nothing will work. I hold to the conviction that something will work because that conviction is important in the lives and destinies of people. People lead in direct relation to the way they experience being led.

If you adopt the philosophy that nothing will work in your church, you have just taught every alcoholic in the church and in the community that nothing will work in his or her struggle with that human hurt and hope. If you adopt the attitude that nothing will work in this church, you have just taught every couple with marriage problems in the church and the community that nothing will work. If you adopt the perspective that nothing will work in this church, you have just taught every young person struggling with his or her own life's direction that nothing will work. Indeed, whenever a church—the key leaders, the pastor, the grass roots members—adopts the philosophy that nothing will work, it has just taught the people in that church and that community who are struggling with any specific hurt and hope that nothing will work in their lives as well.

If, after pooling all of the creative resources available to your local church, you still live the philosophy that nothing will work in this church, you have regrettably taught too many people that nothing will work in their own lives. If nothing will work in something as simple as growing forward a local church, then people regrettably begin to conclude that nothing will work in something as complex as growing forward their lives and destinies.

It is far more decisive and helpful to share with people the spirit of the gospel—something will work. The person struggling with alcoholism, the couple wrestling with their marriage, the young person thinking through the direction of his or her life's destiny, and all people struggling with any specific hurt and hope need the confidence that something will work in their own lives and destinies. And the reason something will work is not because of who we are and what we do, but because of whose we are and what God does.

In Revelation 21:5 we discover these words: "And God who sat upon the throne said, 'Behold, I make all things new' " (RSV). The words do not say, "Behold, I make all things old." The words do not say, "Behold, I make all things the same." The words do not even say, "Behold, you/we make all things new." The words say, "And God . . . said, 'Behold, I make all things new.' "

The reason something will work is because we need only seek to discern the ways in which God is inviting this church forward toward that future God has both promised and prepared for it. The reason something will work is because God takes a hand in the future and destiny of this congregation. The reason something will work is because God goes before the people as a cloud by day and as a fire by night, leading them through this present wilderness to that promised future. The reason something will work is because we are the Easter people. We are the people of the open tomb, the risen Lord, and new life in Christ. Out of that conviction we know that in our lives, even as in our church, something will work.

3. The Major Qualitative Resources for Long-range Planning

Long-range planning is an art, not a skill. Long-range planning invites the best *mutual* wisdom, judgment, vision, common sense, and prayer of all the participants. These are its major qualitative resources. As you draw on these major resources you share in the development of an effective long-range plan that will help you successfully move ahead in your mission.

Effective long-range planning is not finally a matter of gimmicks and gadgets, graphs and charts, tricks and trivialities. Sometimes when I have been asked, "What are the major resources for developing a long-range plan?", the question has had an implicit corollary: "Is there some neat and nifty, quick and easy gimmick someone could learn?" Effective long-range planning is not that simplistic.

Central to the development of an effective long-range plan is the 20–80 principle: 20 percent of the things an organization does yields 80 percent of its results, accomplishments, and achievements. Conversely, 80 percent of what an organization does yields 20 percent of its results. One way to illustrate the 20–80 principle is to consider that two out of ten plays win football games. The art is in selecting the best two plays. Of one hundred objectives your church will work on in the coming three to five years, twenty will deliver 80 percent of the future for your church. In your planning focus on those twenty percenters that will yield 80 percent of the desired results. Discerning which objectives among all those you could do are the twenty percenters requires considerable wisdom, judgment, vision, common sense, and prayer.

The myth in the church is, If people were only more committed and worked harder, things would get better. The truth of the matter is that when people work harder, they get more tired; things don't necessarily get better. When a person who is digging a hole for himself works harder, he or she simply digs a deeper hole. When a church headed in the wrong direction works harder, it simply goes in the wrong direction more quickly.

The art is to work smarter, not harder. Focus only on those twenty percenters that will deliver 80 percent of the future. In the long term this will enable you to work smarter, not harder. You will be in a stronger position to grow forward as an effective and successful church in mission.

As you help a church to develop an effective long-range plan, it is a central, decisive task to nurture forward the group's best wisdom, judgment, vision, common sense, and prayer. You must pool these major qualitative resources to discover the best direction for your church—to discover the few key objectives, the twenty percenters, that will deliver 80 percent of the results.

Over the years I have seen many churches make the regrettable mistake of developing thick, 97-page long-range planning documents. They gather every idea tentatively proposed for probable consideration and discussion. This is what I affectionately call the "cafeteria list" approach to long-range planning. That document accomplishes two excellent things. First, it sits on a shelf that would otherwise be empty. Second, it gathers dust, which would otherwise have to be gathered in some other part of the galaxy.

The best long-range planning documents I see are short—one to three pages or occasionally five to seven pages long. These documents identify and include only the twenty percenters that will deliver 80 percent of the future for that church. To be sure, we will do the eighty percenters each year as they come to us. We will do them with faithfulness and integrity. And they will deliver 20 percent of the results. But none of the eighty percenters are included in an effective long-range plan. An effective long-range plan includes only those twenty percenters that will deliver 80 percent of the results.

This is why effective long-range planning is an art. As leaders you know your church and community best. You have studied the central characteristics of effective churches and the foundational planning principles I have shared in *Twelve Keys to an Effective Church*. Now the art of what you are about is to pool your best wisdom, judgment, vision, common sense, and prayer on behalf of your church's future mission.

Wisdom

I once observed that the primary difference between the two words *no* and *now* is the *w* for *wisdom*. Wisdom is the capacity to discern, understand, and appreciate the dynamics operating in a given group of persons. Wisdom is the capacity to discern the ways in which the dynamics of memory, change, conflict, and hope are distinctively affecting and shaping each "now" event, each "now" in the life and work of a specific local church. (See chapter 13 for a fuller discussion of these four dynamics.) It takes considerable wisdom to discern the ways in which these four dynamics live themselves out in the particular sociological, economic, cultural, vocational, and theological patterns present in a specific local church. It takes wisdom to think through ways one can best help in the light of the specific characteristics of a given local church and community.

Judgment

You are invited to evaluate and develop a realistic assessment of your church's present standing and stature. You are invited to choose the primary direction for your future. You are invited to discover your maximum mission potential. You are invited to decide the number of members, constituents, and persons your church plans to serve in mission each year. You are asked to rate your church's foundational strengths. You are asked to complete rating guides to assess your church's rating for each of the twelve central characteristics.

The art is to exercise judgment, to form an opinion by discerning and comparing—that is, to accurately assess and evaluate where your church stands in relation to each of the twelve central characteristics. It doesn't help to overestimate or to underestimate. Judgment is the capacity to see where you really are.

This invites you to put aside generalizations of where you hope you could be; to put aside sentimental notions of where you wish you could be; and to put aside doom-and-gloom thoughts of how bad you think it might be. You are invited to bring to bear your best judgment to achieve an accurate, thoughtful diagnosis of your realistic strengths and weaknesses. This invites your best mutual judgment.

Vision

Long-range planning invites your best vision—powerful imagination, unusual discernment, foresight. We need vision that is responsible and realistic, not naive and idealistic, vision that is courageous and compassionate, not timid and calculating, vision that is prayerful and powerful, not self-centered and weak.

In developing an effective long-range plan you must compare, think through, and select those few key objectives that will best expand or add specific foundational strengths in your local church. This invites considerable vision. You must see beyond what has been and what is to what can be and what will be.

One of the most decisive watershed questions in long-range planning is, Do you believe your best years are before you or behind you? I have known people in their late eighties, limping on a cane, who are convinced that with God's help some of their best years are before them. And I have also known those people in their early twenties who, sadly, have convinced themselves that their best years are behind them.

It is a self-fulfilling prophecy. Those people—and those churches—convinced that their best years are behind them will not be disappointed. Those churches that look back to the glory years of the churched culture of the 1950s, when their sanctuaries were filled to the brim, have already become has-been churches. Those people and those churches convinced that some of their best years in mission are before them won't be disappointed either. The prophecy fulfills itself. Those churches that look forward to that future in mission that God has both promised and prepared for them will not be disappointed. Some of their best years are before them. This invites our best vision.

Common sense

Sometimes one of the best things a consultant shares with a local church is common sense. Sometimes one of the best things we share with one another is our common sense as to what will work, what can work, what won't work, and what can't work. Common sense is the capacity to fix things that are broken and to recognize that "if it's not broken, don't fix it"—that is, common sense is down-to-earth.

A church that has realistic, common-sense objectives will avoid the dilemma of procrastination. Pure procrastination is not often found in churches. But people do sometimes postpone or put off taking action on objectives. The cause can be traced to their compulsiveness toward perfectionism. When churches set objectives that are unrealistic, grandiose, or glittering with generalities, it is innately clear they cannot be achieved. Most people prefer to succeed, not fail. And so people postpone or put off action when faced with grandiose objectives that they innately sense they will fall short of; they sense they have set themselves up to fail.

Whenever a group has chosen objectives so grandiose and glittering that they cannot be achieved (they are doomed to failure), people procrastinate and postpone action toward those objectives. They also mentally kick themselves for procrastinating. They would be better off kicking themselves for their compulsiveness toward perfectionism. One of the things that counters the compulsiveness toward perfectionism is common sense, making it one of the best qualitative resources for developing an effective long-range plan.

Prayer

One of the best things Christians do is pray together. When we seek to discern those twenty percenters that will deliver 80 percent of the future, the best thing we can do is to pray to God for the best wisdom, judgment, vision, and common sense God can grant us.

It is amazing to me how many churches, when they do long-range planning, act more like amateur sociologists than called-of-God Christians. They never pray. They study reams upon reams of data, as though the more data they study, the more the data will tell them what to do. The truth of the matter is the more data they study, the more confused they become. The data itself does not tell the direction forward.

One of the best things Christians do together is pray. And one of the best things we can do in developing an effective long-range plan is to pray. In Jeremiah 29:11 we discover God's words to the prophet Jeremiah: "For I know the plans I have for you. . . . plans for welfare and not for evil, to give you a future and a hope" (RSV). Let God have a say in his church.

Our real goal is not constructing the future that we want but seeking to discern that future God has both promised and prepared for this church in mission. And we are seeking to have sufficient wisdom, judgment, vision, and common sense to discern and to discover the ways in which God is calling this church to be in mission in its long-range future. That invites our best prayer.

The spirit of our long-range planning sessions should include an attitude of thoughtful and reverent prayer. It is helpful to invite some group in the church to pray on behalf of and for all the participants developing your church's long-range plan. Pray that God's rich, full presence will be manifest in your work together so that the mission of your church will be blessed and enriched.

4. The Four Invitational Questions

Four invitational questions are important in the development of an effective long-range plan. These invitational questions are also helpful in developing an effective life. It is central and decisive that you continue to hold these four questions before yourself and the group as you move through the four stages of long-range planning.

I call these questions *invitational* because they are intended to encourage your reflection and foster your sense of direction. They are not questions intended to be answered on the front end of a long-range planning process with definite precision and conclusive finality. Do not invest extraordinary amounts of time developing answers to these four invitational questions.

Rather, invitational questions are those that the group keeps in mind as it moves through the four stages of developing an effective long-range plan. The questions have a drawing, leading, invitational character. They are the kind of questions to be kept ever before you as you seek to discern with wisdom, judgment, vision, common sense, and prayer the future direction that will be most helpful for your church. The four invitational questions are as follows:

Where are we headed?
What kind of future are we building?
What are our strengths, gifts, and competencies?
What is God calling us to accomplish in mission?

It is important that you share the content and the spirit of these invitational questions with all the participants in the development of the long-range plan for your church. Life is a pilgrimage; and in developing a long-range plan you are deciding the specific direction of your church's pilgrimage in mission for the years to come. This processive, dynamic, developmental, invitational character of long-range planning is important for leaders to understand and share early in the planning process. And when the planning has been completed ask the four invitational questions again—they are still leading you.

The Future toward Which We Are Headed

The first question, Where are we headed? confirms that we can look to the future. The wrong first question would have been, Where have we been? That would have invited us to look to the past. The church that looks to the past does not see God. God is not in the past. God has acted decisively and compassionately, powerfully and gently in the past. And God has moved on to the present and to the future.

The most decisive understanding of God in the Old Testament is that of the God who goes before the people as a cloud by day and a fire by night, leading them toward that future God has both promised and prepared. And the most decisive understanding of God in the New Testament is of the open tomb, the risen Lord, and new life in Christ.

The church that looks to the future sees God. God goes before your church, inviting your church to that future God has both promised and prepared. The question, Where are we headed? confirms that you can take up this invitation.

The Future We Are Building

What kind of future are we building for our families? Our community? Our world? Our church? That is the proper order and sequence of considerations regarding the second question. Something far more important is at stake in developing an effective long-range plan than the simple survival of a given local church.

First, effective long-range planning is concerned with the lives and destinies of your families, your friends, and the many, many people who will be helped by your church in the years to come. Second, effective long-range planning is concerned with the character and quality of life in the community. There is a direct correlation between the strength of the strongest churches in a community and the character and quality of life in that community. The stronger the strongest churches in that community, the stronger the character and quality of life in that community.

Third, effective long-range planning has at stake the sense of peace and justice, of value and betterment of our world. Fourth, effective long-range planning has at stake the future direction and advancement of a specific local church. What rides on effective long-range planning is not something as simple as the survival of a local church. Indeed, those churches that focus their long-range planning on the survival of their church are those churches that have decided to die.

I invite you to a theology of service, not a theology of survival. It is regrettable that too many local churches become involved in long-range planning in order to survive. Move beyond the preoccupation with the three *M*'s—maintenance, money, and membership. The churches that do the best job of long-range planning are those churches that adopt a theology of service, not survival. Those churches see that what rides on the development of an effective long-range plan is the lives and destinies of many, many families, the character and quality of life in the community, the sense of reconciliation, justice, and peace in our world, and the advancement and betterment in mission of this local church.

Our Strengths, Gifts, and Competencies

The third invitational question is, What are our strengths, gifts, and competencies? The church that claims its strengths claims God; the church that claims its strengths claims God's gifts. I am not inviting you to a naive, foolish optimism or a whistling-in-the-dark positive thinking. Rather, I am inviting you to a biblically based, God-centered understanding of life— and of effective long-range planning. The church that claims its strengths claims the ways in which God has been living and moving and working among this congregation for many years. We are who we are, with what strengths, gifts, and competencies we have, as gifts from God.

The church that denies its strengths denies God. The person who denies his or her strengths denies God's gifts. In life's pilgrimage some people suffer from low self-esteem, thinking more poorly of themselves than they have a right to, and in this they deny God—they deny God's gifts. Likewise some churches suffer from low self-esteem and think more poorly of themselves than they have a right to. And they deny God—they deny God's gifts.

You would be amazed at the churches with excellent, experienced pro players at center, right guard, right tackle, right end, and right halfback that develop a long-range plan that runs around a weak left end. You would be amazed at the churches that have excellent, experienced pro leaders in certain central characteristics of an effective church that design their long-range plan to focus on their shortcomings and concerns. They focus on their weaknesses rather than building on their strengths.

The art of long-range planning is to build on your strengths. Do better what you do best. Then you are in a stronger position to tackle your weaknesses and shortcomings.

The four worst "best questions" to consider in developing an effective long-range plan are these:

What are our problems?
What are our needs?
What are our concerns?
What are our weaknesses and shortcomings?

You would be amazed at the number of church planning groups that go off on a retreat each year with enough newsprint to wallpaper three walls and begin their planning by inviting everyone in the room to list their church's problems, needs, concerns, weaknesses, and shortcomings. During the first few hours of the planning retreat they successfully fill three walls of newsprint listing 114 problems, needs, concerns, weaknesses, and shortcomings. And they accomplish three things: a rich, full harvest of despair, a rich, full harvest of depression, and a rich, full harvest of despondency.

Why? I think one reason pastors and key leaders are sometimes attracted to those four questions is that they have their own sense of despair, depression, and despondency. And that is understandable from time to time when someone is engaged in something as complex and ambiguous as being in mission on one of the richest mission fields on the planet. But pastors and key leaders seem attracted, as moths to the flame, to those four worst "best questions." After 114 problems, needs, concerns, weaknesses, and shortcomings have been listed, everybody else in the room has their own full share of despair, depression, and despondency too. Then the despondent pastors and key leaders don't quite feel as bad because everybody else feels a whole lot worse. Misery does sometimes love company.

As a consultant I have been frequently invited to help churches teetering on the brink of the abyss, almost ready to fall into the depths of the chasm below. I am not proposing that we deny or never examine problems, needs, concerns, weaknesses, and shortcomings. But a church that first claims its strengths is in a stronger position to deal with its shortcomings. A church that begins long-range planning with the four worst best questions becomes preoccupied with its problems. And it doesn't see its strengths well enough to build them forward in order to become stronger and thereby move into a better position to tackle its problems, needs, concerns, weaknesses, and shortcomings.

I call these four worst "best questions" the four horsemen of the apocalypse—the four assassins of hope. They lead a church to begin its long-range planning process without God. They lead a church to begin its long-range planning process without recognizing and giving thanks for God's gifts.

The third invitational question is decisively important because it helps a church to begin its long-range planning process by claiming the ways in which God has been living and moving and working in this church for many years. And whatever strengths, gifts, competencies we have, we have as God's gifts. We therefore begin our long-range planning with God.

God's Calling to Mission

The fourth invitational question is, What is God calling us to accomplish in mission? You will note that the question does not ask what we want to do. Fortunately some earlier approaches to long-range planning are now virtually archeological relics. The old "I wish," or "I dream," approach and the "If you had two million dollars, how would you spend it?" approach have nearly faded from the scene. The failure of these approaches is that they all begin with "I." What is decisive in long range planning is, What is *God* calling us to accomplish? It takes wisdom, judgment, vision, common sense, and prayer to discern the nature of God's invitation to this church in the coming three, five, or seven years.

You will note a second implication: the question clearly asks, What is God calling us to *accomplish?* The focus of the question is on accomplishments and achievements, not on activities and doings. We are not living the myth of the busy suburban church of the churched culture of the 1950s, where the task of the church seemed to be to help people become busily involved in a merry-go-round of doings and activities. After all that busyness many churches looked back after several years and wondered what they had accomplished and achieved on behalf of God's cause.

Effective long-range planning focuses on God's invitation to accomplish and achieve on behalf of his mission. The term *mission*, you will note, is the third decisive characteristic of this question. The question asks, What is God calling us to accomplish in mission? not What is God calling us to accomplish in ministry? Unfortunately the term *ministry* has acquired the false connotation that the "real work" of the church is being done by the ordained clergy. Further, the term *ministry* suggests a connotation that we are still living in the churched culture of the 1950s. The truth of the matter is that this is one of the richest mission fields on the planet. Conservatively speaking, 50 percent of the population of this country is effectively unchurched.

When I go to a door and knock on it, and someone comes to the door and says, "Oh, well, we're Presbyterian," I know immediately they are effectively unchurched. If they had come to the door and said, "Oh, we go to First Presbyterian; Rev. Smith is our pastor," I would know they were churched. Whenever a person shares with you primarily a denominational label, you can usually count on that person being effectively unchurched—that is, his or her participation level is minimal at best.

Dr. George Morris, professor of evangelism at Candler School of Theology, Emory University, told me recently of the eight months he lived in central Appalachia. He spent much of that time visiting families, knocking on doors up and down the hollows, ridges, and valleys. Seventy percent of the families he visited were effectively unchurched. Many of those families could not even remember anyone in their family who in their living memory had been Christian—an aunt, a grandfather, a great uncle, or a great grandmother. I was recently in Ohio helping a church, and the pastor mentioned to me the fact that he was formerly a missionary in Africa. And I said to him, "No, my good friend, you are currently a missionary—in Ohio."

What is God calling us to accomplish in mission? God invites us to see that the day of mission is at hand. Those churches that continue to behave as though this were the churched culture of the 1950s will do one thing predictably well—they will become stable and declining or dying churches. Those churches that have discovered that we live on one of the richest mission fields on earth will reach out on behalf of Christ to serve the human hurts and hopes of the countless hundreds upon hundreds of people within average trip time of where their church gathers each Sunday morning. (Average trip time refers to the amount of time people spend in an average trip to work, shopping, or social events.)

Christ at the Door

Some time ago I was helping a church; several of us were in the sanctuary, puzzling and praying as to what would best be helpful in advancing the future mission of that church. Their sanctuary has a remarkable stained glass window of Christ, standing at a door, knocking. The sunlight was coming through the window that day in an amazing way, and it dawned on me what that picture, what that image of Christ means in our time. In the churched culture of the 1950s the understanding was that Christ stood at the door, knocking, hoping someone would come to the door and open the door and invite Christ *in*—to their lives. What that image means in our time, on one of the richest mission fields on the planet, is that Christ stands at the door, knocking, hoping someone will come to the door and open the door so that Christ can invite them *out*—to share his life in mission with the human hurts and hopes of people in our community. It is no longer a matter of us inviting Christ *in*—to our lives. It is now Christ inviting us *out*—to share his life—in mission.

5. What to Listen For and Look For

In developing an effective long-range plan you generate considerable creativity. Many participants share excellent ideas and good suggestions. They also share their best judgment as to the church's strengths, competencies, and gifts and its problems, weaknesses, and shortcomings. The *Planning Workbook* is designed to facilitate a rich, full sharing of these materials. Considerable analysis, diagnosis, data, and possibilities will emerge.

What to Listen For

It is most important that you, other key leaders, your pastor, and all participants in developing the long-range plan have some sense of what to listen for in the midst of all the diagnoses and data. From my years of experience as a consultant I encourage you to listen at three levels.

First, listen for what *is* said. You should listen with considerable thought to precisely what is being said. People have an extraordinary ability to teach you where they are at and what they think. And they do so by what they say.

In one church I served as a consultant a woman raised her hand during the third stage of the process and said, "Dr. Callahan, what we need is a larger choir." Some of the people in the room who sat near the back of the sanctuary on Sunday morning thought she was saying, "What we need is a louder choir," because they themselves had trouble hearing the choir when they sat underneath the overhang of the balcony. The choir director thought she was saying, "What we need is a choir that sings more classical music so that it will be considered among the finer choirs in the city." He thought he was reading between the lines but missed the call on both counts.

But what she actually said was, "We need a larger choir." What she precisely meant was that theirs was a choir of twenty, and she felt it was important that there be at least thirty people in the choir, given the size of the sanctuary and the ways in which a choir of thirty would contribute to the sense of dynamic and inspiring corporate worship. Frequently leaders confuse what they think was said for what was actually said. Or they listen for what they think should have been said. Both of these are grievous mistakes and can finally confuse the development of an effective long-range plan.

Second, listen *between the lines*. People sometimes make statements, tentatively fishing to see if their idea is acceptable or if others will hear between the lines and pick up on what they really want to say. They may feel more free to express what they want to say if one of the leaders indicates that he or she understands what they are trying to say and then restates it more fully.

In one church I served as a consultant the church secretary said, "Sometimes, Dr. Callahan, I think I have been here long enough." In the fuller conversation that followed I discovered that she was really tired of the stressful relationship that had emerged between her and the choir director. In her initial statement she was tentatively fishing to discover whether she could more fully share her own concerns.

Third, listen *for what is not said*. As a consultant I learn as much from what is not said as from the other two guidelines put together. When I am working with a church and we are analyzing corporate, dynamic worship, the fact that nothing is said about the preaching tells me a lot. If nothing is said about the preaching, one can conclude that people think reasonably well of this pastor, see his or her strengths in a variety of ways, and understand that, at least for the moment, preaching is not one of them.

If a group is analyzing pastoral and lay visitation in the community and a good deal is said about the pastor's shepherding and the ways in which he or she is helpful in visitation, one learns a great deal by what is not said about the visitation done by key leaders in that congregation.

These guidelines for listening illustrate the best way to learn about the strengths, competencies, shortcomings, and weaknesses of a church.

What to Look For

In a study of the central characteristics of an effective church, you should first look for those foundational strengths that are

already well in place. Using the chart of the twelve characteristics invites people to look in wholistic, integrative, dynamic
ways at the whole of the twelve characteristics at one time. No
one characteristic stands alone; each relates to some of the other
characteristics on the chart.

People make two mistakes when they look at the chart. First,
they become too concerned about whether their church has all
twelve. Well, it would be fun and helpful if on our football team
we had a first string of all-pro players. But as a matter of fact
the team can be a winning team with nine pro players. Likewise
churches are effective and successful with nine out of the twelve
central characteristics well in place as foundational strengths.

The second mistake people make is to look at the chart and
focus on what your church lacks. If you look first for what you
do not have, you will tend to miss seeing what you do have. At
the first practice of the season the wise coach looks over the
players who have come out for practice and asks, "What do we
have going for us this year? Is this the year of power, blocking,
and a running game, or is this the year of speed, quickness, and
a passing game?" The wise church looks first for what it has
going for it—its strengths, gifts, and competencies.

Second, look for the effects of transitions in pastoral and key
leadership positions. The more rapid the transitions, the more
discontinuity of leadership in the church. And the tougher it is
to develop momentum. Wherever there is an excellent match
between a pastor and a congregation, the most productive years
in that relationship begin in the fifth, sixth, and seventh years.

One church I helped had had an excellent match between
pastor and people from 1920 to 1931. That foundational eleven-
year period provided the strength out of which that church faced
the twists and turns of life's vissicitudes in the following years.
Frequently, wherever one has a solid, strong church team, one
can look back to a time when there was an excellent match well
in place for five, six, seven, or more years.

What transitions in leadership have affected the momentum
and dynamic of your church? I know of a church that has been
in existence for 93 years and has had 37 pastors. One can imagine something of the transitions of leadership that occurred in
that church. Discontinuity, disruptiveness, competitiveness, and
a climate of lack of trust contribute considerably to and result
from a high turnover in both the pastoral and key leadership of

a church. It is important to think through how one might bring about and keep in place the rich, full benefits of a good match between key leaders, pastor, and people.

Third, look for those strong, hope-fulfulling events that inform this church's life and sense of future. In the case of one congregation way back in 1886 some of their deepest longings and hopes were dramatically fulfilled in a decisive event. In 1887, 1888, 1889, and every year since then they have celebrated that event in which some of their deepest longings and hopes were decisively fulfilled. Look for the hope-fulfilling events that inform a church and give it a sense of identity, continuity, and fulfilled hope as it looks to the future.

Fourth, look for and understand those traumatic events that have marred and scarred a congregation's life together. In one church during one year four couples—some of the church's leaders—went through the pain and disruption of separation. Some individuals were involved with other people. There were four divorces and finally three remarriages. That year was one of the most traumatic, bizarre, difficult years in the life of that church. People are still building forward their life as a congregation, silently hoping that nothing like that is going to happen again. The scar is twenty years old, and it seems to be well healed, but it can't be erased completely. In another congregation an excellent choir director, for whatever reason, has moved to another part of the country, and it is in relation to that move and the trauma of that beloved choir director's departure that certain things no longer happen in this church in the rich, full way in which they used to.

Finally, look and listen for the influences of everyday, ordinary life. Sometimes we put on "church glasses" and only view those programs and activities that are directly a part of a church's work and mission. As a matter of fact hope-fulfilling events and traumatic events that occur in the everyday lives of people in a congregation decisively affect and shape what is going on in that congregation.

Frequently these events occur among the informal relational neighborhood networks of a congregation. People in our time live in three neighborhoods: a relational neighborhood, a sociological neighborhood, and a geographical neighborhood. More often than not churches tend to focus on the geographical neighborhood and miss both the informal relational neighborhood network and the sociological neighborhood. Listen for and look for what is taking place, has recently taken place, and will likely be taking place in the relational neighborhood networks that are strongly a part of the life and work of this congregation.

You will facilitate the accomplishment of an effective long-range plan by nurturing forward a sensitivity to what to listen for and what to look for, so that you come to a better self-understanding of who you are and of who you will be. This will immeasurably advance the effectiveness of the long-range plan you develop.

6. Principles for Participation

Many people use the nine principles discussed in this chapter to maximize their participation in long-range planning. Your use of these principles will increase your own participation and contributions. Many churches use these principles to advance the quality and quantity of their church's participation. The more persons who are aware of these principles, the more constructive your church's planning and sense of direction. Further, these principles are helpful guidelines as you think through who to select to give leadership as your church develops its own long-range plan. The more fully these nine principles are followed, the more likely your church is to develop an effective long-range plan for its future.

Principle 1. Encourage a Wholistic and Integrative Perspective

Encourage every person who participates in the church's long-range planning to have a wholistic and integrative perspective, not a segmentalist and departmental view. Each person needs to serve as a leader of the whole, not a representative of the parts. Participants in the development of an effective long-range plan should have sufficient distance on each of the parts and a genuine, authentic capacity to view the church as wholistic, integrative, and dynamic rather than to see it only as segmentalist and departmentalized.

As you refer to various charts on the twelve central characteristics in *Twelve Keys to an Effective Church* and *Twelve Keys: The Planning Workbook*, you will see that the charts invite everyone to look at the twelve central characteristics of an effective church with a wholistic, integrative, dynamic perspective rather than a segmentalist, departmental, compartmentalized perspective. Each participant should be encouraged to nurture this capacity to see the whole.

If there is any serious mistake people make in developing a long-range plan, it is that they bring together people who are leaders or advocates of various segments and departments within the church and then ask them to try to look at the whole. In my experience I have seen how it is sometimes difficult for a leader or an advocate of some specific segment or department to focus on the whole. Indeed, that person has already been giving leadership in some segmented department of the church's work and will tend to continue to focus on that department.

When a long-range planning group consists only of representatives of various departments, they will tend to find themselves in the old dilemma of being unable to see the forest for the trees. Everybody comes to the long-range planning task because he or she is representing some "tree." Each advocate brings his or her own tree to the table, intending to assure that it receives its share of water. The group develops a good give and take. Everyone cooperates genuinely in coordinating a plan that gives each tree its fair share of water. But the group is so preoccupied with representing each specific segment and department and protecting individual "turf" in the long-range plan that members have difficulty seeing the whole forest they might be able to grow forward.

It is not helpful to select for this planning task people who have a vested interest in a specific segment and compartment of the church's work. Encourage people to see the whole.

Principle 2. Develop a Long-Range Focus

The best leadership in the development of an effective long-range plan comes from those people able to perceive a long-range time horizon rather than an annual time horizon. Frequently people in a congregation who do not participate in a specific departmental leadership task have a mentor's capacity to look at the whole in long-range ways. Precisely this kind of person is important to include in the development of the long-range plan.

Those who participate in developing the long-range plan should have the capacity to look three, five, seven, or ten years ahead. Look for people who, in their day-to-day work, develop future plans and consider the long-range view of things. These people generally have the experience and skills in looking ahead to long-range time horizons. These people can distinguish the long-range, important issues from the short term, urgent issues.

There is a difference between *important* and *urgent*. Important objectives have significant worth and consequence. They are twenty percenter objectives. Urgent objectives call for immediate attention. Encourage people to look in long-range ways at the important, not the urgent, key objectives. Over the long term these will be the twenty percenters that deliver 80 percent of the results.

Some people have a tendency to focus on urgent, but not important issues. They are looking for activities that deliver quick closure, short-term, immediate satisfaction results. These people will not give the best leadership in long-range planning. And certainly you would not want a person who gets easily sidetracked by things that are neither important nor urgent. Encourage people to focus on important, long-range issues.

To be sure, churches develop an effective long-range plan in order to know what makes best sense to achieve today. The purpose of long-range planning is not solely so a congregation can be where it wants to be in the coming years. You decide where you want to be in the long run precisely so you will know what makes sense to achieve today and tomorrow. It takes this long-range focus to develop an effective plan for your church. Look to where you want to be so you will know what makes sense to do now.

Principle 3. Encourage a Processive and Dynamic View

Encourage every participant to develop a processive and dynamic perspective of long-range planning, not a block and static view. Effective long-range planning is ongoing and productive, focused on an end result.

An old way of doing long-range planning was to choose a specific time horizon, such as five years, and develop a long range plan for that block of time. It isolated smaller blocks of time as year 1, year 2, year 3, year 4, and year 5. It steadfastly moved sequentially through each of the blocks for all five years of the plan, looking neither right nor left to evaluate, revise, change, or improve. That block and static understanding is less helpful in our time.

The better way forward is for your church to select whatever time horizon makes best sense to it—three, five, seven, or ten years—and then to develop a processive, dynamic approach to its long-range planning. For example, the best time horizon for a specific local church might be five years. In the current year, using the *Planning Workbook*, the local church selects central characteristics to expand and to add, along with specific key objectives related to each of those central characteristics, and sets a timeline for the coming five years.

During the first year of the five-year plan the church works creatively and constructively toward the accomplishment of its key objectives for the first year. Then, toward the end of the first year, the church does two things (1) it evaluates, modifies, improves, and advances the key objectives for the next four years, and (2) it adds new timelines and key objectives for one more year, the new "fifth" year. The church using a five-year plan should always be processively and dynamically working five years ahead.

To be sure, on some objectives the church may be working as many as ten or fifteen years ahead. But in foundational, fundamental ways it focuses on the emerging five years. This approach has considerable merit over the old static approach. First, it gives the local church the opportunity to evaluate, modify, improve, and advance its key objectives toward the end of each year. Second, it gives the church the chance to add timelines and key objectives for the new next year in ways that contribute to the rhythm of momentum and dynamic the church is developing. Thus you want to nurture persons to think in processive and dynamic ways so their participation will be most helpful in developing your church's long-range plan.

Principle 4. Limit the Amount of Time for Planning

Encourage every person who participates in developing your church's long-range plan to limit the amount of time he or she is willing to invest in long-range planning. Indeed, look for people willing to limit the amount of time they will invest in developing an effective long-range plan.

One of the major mistakes churches make is to assume that a limitless amount of time is available for planning. Some churches have even had long-range planning committees in existence for several years and have yet to put one key objective down on paper. Just because you are working in long-range terms does not mean you have an unlimited amount of time to develop a plan.

Dr. Merrill Douglass, an excellent leader and friend, leads many of the American Management Association's seminars on time management. He has coined a phrase, Douglass's Law of Clutter: Clutter expands to fill the space available. I have coined my own phrase, Callahan's Law of Planning: Planning expands to fill the time available. Therefore, limit the amount of time you invest in planning.

The *Planning Workbook* is designed to help you lead six major sessions of long-range planning. At the conclusion of those six sessions you will have selected the key objectives that are your twenty percenters, using your best wisdom, judgment, vision, common sense, and prayer. Then a year from now, toward the end of the first year of your long-range plan, move quickly through these six sessions again in an evaluative and planning process. Look for any helpful modifications, changes, improvements, and advances over what you had in place and add key objectives and timelines for the new next year in your plan.

Limit the amount of time you are willing to invest in planning. As a result you will be more likely to center on twenty percenters. The more time people allow for planning, the more often they succumb to preoccupation with details, leading to analysis paralysis. The more time people allow for planning, the more often they dawdle with objectives that are really eighty percenters and that detract from rich, full discussion of those few twenty percenters that will best advance the future of their church. Regrettably some people assume that the more time they spend in planning, the more commitment they are demonstrating. They are simply demonstrating they do not know how to plan well. Encourage people to limit the amount of time they will invest in long-range planning.

Principle 5. Share Your Wisdom

Help every person who participates to share his or her best wisdom, judgment, vision, common sense, and prayer and help him or her to nurture these qualities in the other participants. Be concerned with fostering the unique strengths of your church, not with conforming to conventional notions of what a church should be.

For example, some planning groups become preoccupied with demographics. Some become involved in what I sometimes call the "demographic captivity" of the church. Historically there was the Babylonian captivity of the people of Israel. In the 1950s there emerged the "suburban captivity" of the church—the myth that to be effective and successful as a church, one had to look like a busy, successful, suburban church of the 1950s. Regrettably rural churches, inner-city churches, village churches, county seat churches, large downtown churches, neighborhood churches, and regional churches tried to follow suit. They became preoccupied with trying to mimmick the busy suburban churches of that time. They stopped doing what they did best. To this day some people assume that when we start a new church it is best to create a busy suburban church of the 1950s.

The Christian faith survived and moved forward in its mission for more than nineteen hundred years without ever knowing what a busy suburban church (a la 1950s) looked like. Fortunately we have almost grown beyond the suburban captivity of the church. Yet we are still involved in the demographic captivity of the church. There is no direct correlation between population growth and church growth. Churches exist all over the country that are stable and declining or dying amid growing populations. They are not delivering nine out of the twelve central characteristics.

By contrast churches exist all over the country that are stable and growing amid declining populations. They are delivering nine out of the twelve central characteristics of an effective church. And even when the population in that county or township has declined over the past twenty years, the percentage of the total population that is effectively unchurched has substantially increased—that church is growing because it is reaching its fair share of the effectively unchurched population in that county or township.

When I am in the southeast, church members tell me if it weren't for all of the Southern Baptists, they would be doing better. When I am on the West Coast, people there tell me if it weren't for all the nondenominational churches, they would be doing better. When I am in the northeast church members there tell me if it weren't for all of the Roman Catholics, they would be doing better. Some time ago, while helping a church near Boston, I visited a Roman Catholic priest. And he said to me, "You know, Dr. Callahan, if it weren't for all the Congregationalists, we'd be doing better."

It's almost as if the phrase is "If it weren't for all the _(fill in the blank)_, we'd be doing better." The truth of the matter is, the largest "denomination" in the country is the denomination of the unchurched. The truth of the matter is, the demographics have some bearing, but not a decisive, final bearing. Can you imagine Paul on the dock at Corinth, watching the sail of the ship on the horizon, eagerly and expectantly waiting there at the dock for that ship to bring to him the latest demographic printouts from the computer in Rome so he would know where to go next to witness to the gospel?

I do want to affirm that demographic study has its important place. For years I have taken into consideration the demographic data of countless communities across this country. At the same time it is most important that the demographic data not enslave us to a future that someone else has projected. You must focus your best mutual wisdom, judgment, vision, common sense, and prayer on that future God has both promised and prepared for your church in mission. Encourage participants to have that quality and spirit about their lives.

Principle 6. Use "Yes" Voting

The principle of "yes" voting helps to limit the amount of time spent planning and focus the planning group's best wisdom, judgment, vision, common sense, and prayer. The principle is especially helpful in the sixth planning session, when you select the key objectives that will best expand and add the specific central characteristics that constitute the major priorities for your church.

In the fifth planning session the planning teams share their best wisdom as to which central characteristics to expand and add. The results of the planning teams' recommendations are tabulated. Generally the consensus of the planning group is clear as to the specific central characteristics to expand and add. In the fifth planning session the planning group also constructs a timeline for the advancement of these specific central characteristics. Then, between the fifth and sixth planning sessions, each planning team is invited to mull over the few key objectives that will best advance the specific central characteristics that are the major priorities for the church.

When the whole planning group gathers for the sixth session, each planning team is invited to put in place the key objectives it plans to recommend for each specific central characteristic chosen as a major priority. To be sure, each planning team is invited to focus on only two to four key objectives for each "expand" and no more than four to six key objectives for each "add."

Then each planning team is invited to share its best recommendations with the group as a whole. While this is being done leaders should help consolidate comparable recommendations. If one planning team has already suggested a key objective and several other planning teams share comparable key objectives, then it is helpful to consolidate these into one rather than to list them separately.

Even when you have consolidated the key objectives from all the planning teams, sometimes you will still have more than two to four key objectives listed for an "expand" and more than four to six key objectives for an "add." At this juncture, rather than voting yes or no on each key objective related to a specific central characteristic, use the principle of "yes" voting. When multiple options are under consideration "yes" voting permits a positive, affirmative method of selecting the optimum choices. In "yes" voting each voting group is allotted a quantity of votes they may cast in a ballot. Each group is allotted a number of votes equal to half of the total number of options under consideration, plus one more. If eight options are being considered, each group is allotted four votes, plus one more—for a total of five votes. If eleven options are being considered, each group is allotted six votes, plus one more—for a total of seven votes.

Then when votes are tabulated some few options may have a clear majority of the votes, and if this is the case, the voting can stop after the one ballot. When there is not a clear majority the procedure is to take the top 60 percent—that is, in this example, the six out of ten that received the highest number of votes—and use the principle of "yes" voting again with a reduced number of votes.

For example, a planning group has decided to expand the central characteristic of corporate, dynamic worship. In the sixth session the various planning teams have recommended a total of ten key objectives to do so. To be sure, the ten represent a consolidation of comparable key objectives. The group is looking for the best two to four from among these ten. In this example each planning team is given six votes—that is, five, or half the number of options, plus one more. Each planning team is invited to cast its six votes for the key objectives it thinks will be most helpful. Often four of the key objectives emerge as having the strongest consensus of the group.

If that does not happen, take the key objectives in the top 60 percent—the six of the ten that received the highest number of votes—and use the principle of "yes" voting a second time. In this example each planning team would then have four votes—three votes because that represents half of the six, plus one more. Once a vote is taken select the four key objectives that have the highest number of votes as the best key objectives to expand the central characteristic of corporate, dynamic worship.

Do not turn "yes" voting into "no" voting. In our example someone may suggest that time would be saved if, in the original voting on the ten key objectives, every team had four no votes rather than six yes votes. Under that scheme each team would vote against the four they did not want. Do not do that. The time saved will not make up for the momentum lost. It is far more constructive and creative for the planning teams to be voting in favor of what they are *for* than voting for what they would be against.

The principle of "yes" voting is helpful in advancing the constructive, creative character of the sixth planning session. It is an excellent principle to use whenever a group is considering multiple options. In straightforward, constructive ways it helps the group discover the consensus of its best wisdom, judgment, vision, and common sense.

Principle 7. Select a Steering Committee of Five to Twelve Persons

Select five to twelve persons to serve as the long-range planning steering committee that will help your congregation to move through the four stages and six planning sessions in *The Planning Workbook*. Limit the size of the committee to a workable, functioning group that will concentrate primarily on helping key leaders and grass roots of the congregation to develop an effective long-range plan. More often than not the most effective long-range planning steering committee has five to eight persons on it. On occasion I have seen effective committees with as many as twelve persons.

It is important to distinguish the long-range planning steering committee from the long-range planning committee. Every person who participates in the four stages and six sessions is, in reality, part of the long-range planning committee per se. The more participants on the long-range planning committee, the better the results and the more powerful the action, implementation, and momentum. To assist the long-range planning committee it is valuable to have a long-range planning steering committee. Sometimes this group is referred to as the long-range planning task force or as the futuring committee. By whatever name this group has the task of facilitating the widest participation possible from among the congregation in the development of an effective long-range plan. It is not the purpose of this group to decide the long-range plan. The focus of the long-range planning steering committee is to give leadership as the congregation develops an effective long-range plan. The members of this team serve as major resource people with the congregation. They are the "resident experts" on the principles and materials in *Twelve Keys to an Effective Church, Twelve Keys: The Planning Workbook,* and *Twelve Keys: The Leaders' Guide.*

Frequently I am asked to suggest the optimal number of people to include on the long-range planning committee and the long-range planning steering committee for a given size of church. The best way forward is to use average worship attendance, not membership, as the baseline for this decision. Average worship attendance is a better indicator of your realistic size, strength, and vitality. Include a sufficient number of people on the long-range planning committee to have strong links, influence, and impact with the people who are the actual participating congregation of your church. Table 2 is a helpful guide.

The rule of thumb is to include on the long-range planning committee the number of people equal to 20 percent of your average worship attendance (AWA). To be sure, if your AWA is unusually low, for whatever reason, you may want to choose a higher percentage. At the same time the steering committee should be commensurate in size with your long-range planning committee. The proportional sizes in table 2 should be helpful as guidelines. Develop the size of the long-range planning

Table 2. Average Worship Attendance and Appropriate
Committee Sizes

Average Worship Attendance	Number of People[a] on Long-range Planning Committee	Number of People[b] on Long-range Planning Steering Committee
500+	100	12
400	80	12
300	60	8
200	40	8
100	20	5
50	15	5

[a]This range of people would serve as the long-range planning committee
and participate in all six planning sessions.
[b]This range of people would serve as the steering committee to help the
long-range planning committee and congregation achieve an effective long-
range plan.

committee—in relation to the size of your participating congregation—that best shares creative, constructive wisdom, judgment,
vision, and common sense as you prayerfully develop your long-
range plan. And select an excellent steering committee that will
help this to happen.

Sometimes a steering committee gets bogged down and develops analysis paralysis. I have seen local churches whose steering committees have been meeting for three years without developing a sense of long-range planning direction. Why?
Sometimes it is because they are facing complex issues that de-
serve the help of a consultant. Sometimes their lack of progress
is due to one or more of the followings:

- There are too many people on the steering committee, and
  as a result it may try to do the work *for* the congregation
  rather than to work *with* the congregation.
- The committee has seen itself as a "process only" group.
- The committee has seen itself as deciding—dictating—by
  itself the long-range plan. This is the other extreme from
  the "process only" approach. Both are wrong.

An excellent long-range planning steering committee accomplishes three major purposes:

1. Its members serve as excellent resource people for the principles and materials in *Twelve Keys to an Effective Church* and in *Twelve Keys: The Leaders' Guide*.
2. Its members facilitate participation, excellent, creative ideas, and good suggestions from the long-range planning committee, the church's key leaders, and the grass roots, using *Twelve Keys: The Planning Workbook*.
3. Its members share their own best wisdom, judgment, vision, common sense, and prayer straightforwardly and directly; leaders do not process only, nor dictate but lead in solid, strong, corporate ways.

All three of these purposes are necessary. The team shares its own best wisdom as to the way forward and nurtures forward the best thinking of the congregation as well. A long-range planning steering committee of five to twelve persons is more likely to achieve this than a steering committee that has too many members.

Frequently a steering committee of five persons shares its work in the following way:

Person(s)	Resource and Leadership Responsibility	
1	Stage 1	Realistic assessment
1	Stage 2	Primary direction
1	Stage 3	Relational characteristics
1	Stage 3	Functional characteristics
1	Stage 4	Key objectives, timelines

An eight-person steering committee may share its work as follows:

Person(s)	Resource and Leadership Responsibility	
1	Stage 1	Realistic assessment
1	Stage 2	Primary direction
1	Stage 3	Mission, visitation
1		Worship, groups
1		Leadership, decision making, program
1		Accessibility, visibility, parking
1		Facilities, finances
1	Stage 4	Key objectives, timelines

A steering committee of twelve persons may share its work as follows:

Person(s)	Resource and	Leadership Responsibility
1	Stage 1	Realistic assessment
1	Stage 2	Primary direction
2	Stage 3	Mission, visitation
2		Worship, groups
1		Leadership, decision making
2		Program, finances
1		Accessibility, visibility
1		Facilities, parking
1	Stage 4	Key objectives, timelines

It is important to confirm that these are three illustrations; the variety and combinations are considerable. Decide the best way for your church's steering committee to share its resource and leadership responsibilities.

Each person on the long-range planning steering committee should be familiar with *Twelve Keys to an Effective Church* and *Twelve Keys: The Leaders' Guide*. At the same time each person on the steering committee should select a primary resource and leadership responsibility. In this way the five- to twelve-person steering committee gives excellent leadership in helping the long-range plan for your church to move forward.

Principle 8. Select a Steering Committee with a Balance of Strengths

The long-range planning steering committee should have a balance of complementary strengths. Four kinds of strengths are helpful to have present on the steering committee: (1) leading and caring, (2) supporting and giving, (3) analytical and diagnostic, and (4) social and relational. Were the long-range planning steering committee to consist of eight persons, it might be helpful to have one or two persons who are predominantly strong leaders. Two or three persons would provide good follow-up and supporting, giving qualities. One or two persons would bring analytical and diagnostic qualities, and two or three persons would bring social and relational qualities. See table 3 for examples of committees with a balance of strengths. Table 4 lists committees with imbalances that will impair their effectiveness.

It is worth noting that a steering committee of eight, six of whom are strong leaders (see E in table 4) will have rich, full discussions—and there will be a good deal of head knocking

Table 3. Steering Committees that Share a Balance of Strengths

	Committee A	Committee B	Committee C	Committee D
People with Leading and Caring Strengths	2	2	1	2
People with Supporting and Giving Strengths	2	1	3	2
People with Analytical and Diagnostic Strengths	2	3	2	3
People with Social and Relational Strengths	2	2	2	1
Total People	8	8	8	8

and competitive development of each point of view. But that group will likely falter in carrying out follow-through or facilitating the six planning sessions with the congregation. Likewise a committee consisting primarily of supportive, follow-through people (see F in table 4) will be very eager to be helpful but will tend to lack direction, analysis, or links to the congregation.

A committee of eight, six of whom have strong analytical and diagnostic strengths (see G in table 4) will develop an excellent analysis and diagnosis but will falter when it comes to making a decision, carrying out follow-through, or establishing links to the congregation. Moreover, a committee consisting primarily of social and relational persons (see H in table 4) will have an excellent time together—indeed, it will be an excellent party— and they will have strong marvelous links to the congregation,

Table 4. **Steering Committees that Will Be Dysfunctional**

	Committee E	Committee F	Committee G	Committee H
People with Leading and Caring Strengths	6	–	–	–
People with Supporting and Giving Strengths	1	5	1	2
People with Analytical and Diagnostic Strengths	1	1	6	1
People with Social and Relational Strengths	–	2	1	5
Total People	8	8	8	8

but whether they can give leadership to the congregation's long-range planning is open to question.

The best steering committee consists of a team of persons who bring complementary strengths to the task. The long-range planning steering committee with a balance of complementary strengths is more likely to facilitate the congregation's best participation in developing an effective long-range plan.

Principle 9. Seek Links with the Congregation.

Those on the long-range planning steering committee should be people whom the grass roots of the congregation view with a sense of mutual trust, respect, integrity, credibility, and confidence. Give thoughtful weight to considering the view the grass roots of the congregation has of this person. Do not look to please the pastor or key leaders here. People whom the congregation respects and trusts are important to include as part of the steering committee.

These people, as participants on the steering committee, will have strong links with the congregation, not so much programmatic nor power links but informal and relational links of mutual trust and respect. Such links tend to bring forth a rich, full dialogue both informally and formally and result in sharing between the grass roots of the congregation, the key leaders, and the steering committee.

The *Planning Workbook* invites the long-range planning steering committee to lead the long-range planning committee and the congregation through the four major stages of long-range planning in six planning sessions. It is *not* the purpose of long-range planning to force the whole congregation to participate in the development of an effective long-range plan. The input to the six sessions of long-range planning will be distorted if people feel that they have been legalistically driven to be present.

The best way forward is to describe the four major stages of long-range planning and the six planning sessions in an invitational, community way, so that people look forward to participating and sharing their excellent ideas and good suggestions. The steering committee should include as many congregation members as possible in the four stages so they can share their excellent ideas, good suggestions, evaluation, and analysis with one another and with the steering committee. Each person who participates in the planning sessions will benefit from having his or her own *Planning Workbook* with which to share and discuss as the team partners put into place their best thinking for the future of their church.

The more links people on the steering committee have with the congregation, the more likely congregation members are to participate in the planning process with that spirit. And it is most important that the planning sessions be done in a relaxed, sharing, and caring way, not in a tense, legalistic, judgmental way. People are more likely to discover creative new ideas in a relaxed and enjoyable series of sessions. The links with the congregation that the steering committee has will facilitate this spirit in the planning sessions.

Part Two

RESOURCES FOR ACTION, IMPLEMENTATION, AND MOMENTUM

7. An Effective Long-range Plan

Seven qualities contribute to a local church having a strong track record of action, implementation, and momentum. Churches without these seven qualities generally do not have a strong track record. Regrettably such churches have become preoccupied with meetings and coordination, indecision and analysis paralysis, inertia and impassivity. As you give leadership to your church, think through which of these seven qualities are already present and which ones can be nurtured forward as you move toward your church's future. The seven qualities are as follows:

1. An effective long-range plan
2. An excellent match of leaders and key objectives
3. An excellent match of motivational resources between key leaders, the pastor, and the grass roots of the congregation
4. Leadership development that focuses on the "middle third," the middle range of competence.
5. Recognition of the value of excellent mistakes
6. Recognition that some key objectives are worth not doing
7. A prayer life that has about it the qualities of vision and hope

This chapter and the remaining chapters in part 2 discuss these qualities in depth. The first quality, an effective long-range plan, can be characterized in terms of the five criteria it must meet.

Criterion 1. The plan includes only the twenty percenters

An effective long-range plan includes only those twenty percenters that yield 80 percent of the results. Whenever even one or two eighty percenters creep in, that long-range plan loses effectiveness. The inclusion of even one or two eighty percenters gives rise to yet a third and then a fourth. They multiply almost like dandelions—once one or two get in, before you know it there are ten or fifteen. The best long-range plans I see include only those twenty percenters that will deliver 80 percent of the results. Think through whether or not each key objective being considered for your long-range plan represents a twenty percenter.

Criterion 2. The plan matches with current strengths

A long-range plan is effective when the central characteristics you plan to expand and add match well with your church's current strengths. Too many churches develop long-range plans that shore up their weaknesses rather than build on their strengths. The art of developing an effective long-range plan is in selecting one or two of the current foundational strengths among the twelve central characteristics that can be expanded. The expansion of those current strengths helps set up the church to succeed, not fail. It helps the church to develop a sense of momentum.

The next step is to select one or two new central characteristics you want to build forward into strengths—to add new strengths that match well with the strengths already well in place. The long-range planning process that puzzles this through in wholistic, integrative, dynamic ways can be expected to result in the development of an effective long-range plan.

Criterion 3. The plan matches with the community and mission field the church seeks to serve

As your group thinks about expanding and adding central characteristics, look for a fitting match with the community and with the mission field your church seeks to serve. After considering the large number of gray-haired people in the congregation, a church in Florida once decided that the future of the church was at stake. So the church invested $1.3 million in building a gymnasium to attract youth so that it would survive after the older people were gone. That gym sits empty most of the time.

If this church had matched its central characteristics with the community and mission field it served, leaders would have realized that the future of the church was not endangered. The new "youth" who will see to the ongoing future of that church in the coming twenty-five years are retiring in Indiana, Ohio, Pennsylvania, and New York at sixty-five years of age. They are moving to the south and settling in that part of Florida and will continue to do so over the coming quarter of a century. That church would have been better off developing specific, concrete missional objectives and several competent programs that focused on recently retired people rather than on youth. That would have constituted a better match in terms of the community and mission field available to that church.

Criterion 4. The plan depends on the plays the players can run

A long-range plan is effective when it sends in the plays the players can run—when its key objectives are those the leadership team can accomplish. Too many churches try to fit their key objectives and their leadership team into the already existing organizational structure of their denomination.

The art is to never send in plays the players cannot run. The art is to never send in more plays than the players can run. An effective long-range plan has a reasonable number of objectives that match best with the players, the leadership team, and the strengths, gifts, and competencies with which God has blessed them.

Form follows function. Structure follows strategy. Organization follows objectives. The proper order is (1) select your key objectives, (2) do so in relation to your key leaders, and (3) shape your organizational structure to match. Too many churches do it the other way around. Include just enough people on just enough committees that wise decisions are achieved and significant results are accomplished. And shape the structure to help, not hinder, the team.

Criterion 5. The plan does not set too many objectives

The fifth criterion of an effective long-range plan is built on the Callahan Principle: Plan less to achieve more. Do not focus on more central characteristics than can reasonably be accomplished within your specified time horizon. The art is to focus on the few decisive central characteristics and the related key objectives that will best expand or add those characteristics.

Some churches assume that the more key objectives, the better the plan. Some churches assume that the more pages to their planning document, the better the plan. As a matter of fact the more pages included, the fewer the people who will use the plan.

Long-range planning tends to expand to fill the time available. Long-range plans tend to expand to fill the number of sheets of paper available. Limit the time, limit the number of sheets of paper, and limit the number of key objectives. Then your church can focus on only those twenty percenters that match your current strengths, the community and mission field you serve, and the leadership team available. Keep the spirit that you plan to select a few key objectives and achieve them. That creates the dynamic of spillover impact on the work and mission of your church.

I learned a long time ago in coaching basketball that the art is to help each player discover his or her best shot. When the players practice shooting they focus on their best shot, so that seven out of ten times, as the ball leaves their hands, they have both the confidence and the competence that the ball is going in the basket. This increases the probability that, when they get the ball in another part of the court, their competence and confidence will spill over and they will be more likely to make the shot. The players who practice shots all over the court and never focus on improving their best shot end up with mediocre shooting records. Those who focus on their best shots grow forward an excellent team and a strong track record of action, implementation, and momentum.

8. Leaders and Key Objectives

Churches with a strong track record of action, implementation, and momentum do an excellent job of matching leaders and key objectives. If there is any mistake that most local churches make, it is that they tend to match people who are willing—but who will not do the job well—with specific key objectives. The art is to match key objectives with people who will do the job well, not those who are simply willing.

Establishing an Excellent Match

In choosing objectives in your planning choose those with tasks that you and your leaders can do. In choosing people to work on tasks choose those who can do them well, not those who are willing. Being willing to work is different from being able to do a task well.

Once, as a coach of a church softball team, I had occasion to apply these principles. All season long one of my players had jumped up and down during practice, saying, "Let me pitch, coach, let me pitch!" In this particular game I had decided to give him a chance to pitch. One of the hardest things I have had to do as a coach was to walk out to the mound in the first inning when we were nine runs behind, there were no outs, and the bases were loaded. I said to the pitcher, "Good friend, it is my mistake. I should have been out here five runs ago. You are our best shortstop. Please go and play shortstop. Sam is coming in as pitcher. With your fielding, the rest of the team's fielding, and Sam's pitching, we will get out of this inning and beyond this game."

Some people are willing to do pastoral and lay visitation but do not do it well, even if they go out to visit week after week. You cannot assume that if they had a bit more commitment and worked harder, somehow their visitation would get better. They will do more harm than good to their own spiritual growth pilgrimage and to the spiritual growth of the persons they visit. Instead choose people who are competent to do the visitation well.

The art is to match people with objectives so that the objectives can be reached. The biblical narrative is quite clear on the diversity of human gifts. People have various strengths, gifts, and competencies and can accomplish certain tasks with an extraordinary degree of achievement. When we match a person with some other task that he or she does not do well, we deny his or her real gifts. The art is to help people to discover those strengths, gifts, and competencies with which God has blessed their lives—and to match those competencies with tasks related to a key objective so that people can put their gifts and competencies to work in ways that count. They will have a high level of satisfaction in seeing their work come to fruition.

Churches with a strong track record of action, implementation, and momentum do *not* focus on getting people to fill slots where the church needs a body. Instead these churches focus on helping people to discover where their specific gifts and competencies can best be shared. They focus not on where the church needs help. They focus on where each person can best help. They see people as unique resources rather than as a means to fill the church's momentary needs. They help each person to match his or her competencies to the most appropriate key objectives.

Developing Excellent Job Descriptions

One important factor in establishing an excellent match between leaders and key objectives is to develop an excellent job description with each key leader. Excellent job descriptions help your church's key leaders to develop successfully in their tasks. Such a job description includes the following components:

- Two to four key objectives to be accomplished
- Major responsibilities
- Range of authority
- Lines of accountability
- One to two competencies to be developed
- Job description details
- Steps for evaluation and improvement

Two to Four Key Objectives

These objectives, which this person looks forward to achieving, should be spelled out, and they should match well with the specific central characteristics your church is planning to expand or add. Each key leader should consider this question: What are the two to four key objectives I look forward to achieving by the end of the coming year? Clearly stated objectives help each key leader to focus on putting them well in place, in keeping with the criteria for an excellent objective.

The Major Responsibilities

Many churches make the mistake of handing leaders a long list of activities and doings that immediately places those leaders on a merry-go-round of busyness. A good job description lists those major responsibilities a person must fulfill in order to achieve the two to four objectives they need to accomplish. Certain major responsibilities are inherent in achieving specific objectives. Too many key leaders have not had the chance to think through what their major responsibilities are.

The Range of Authority

It is important to delegate authority to people along with responsibility. Never give responsibility without also granting authority. There are three areas of responsibility for which authority should be clearly spelled out: leadership, decision making, and financial resources. This can be done by setting clear guidelines as follows:

- List the groups, committees, task forces, and persons appropriately and directly accountable to this person,
- State the range of decisions this person has the authority to make;
- Detail the range of financial resources this person has available.

Accountability

Each leader should appreciate and understand to whom he or she is accountable. Straight-line accountability is far better than multiple-line accountability.

Specific Competencies to Be Developed

Help each leader to identify the one or two competencies he or she plans to enhance and develop during the coming year. This is an often-overlooked component of a good job description. Help each leader be in a proactive, growing, building, and developing stance during the coming year.

The Job Description Details

List any details related to a leadership position that would be helpful to a new person coming to this task. Job description details include such things as hours of work, commitments to meetings, and available resources. For staff positions, this section would also include the salary and other forms of compensation.

Evaluation and Improvement

Each job description should include a process for evaluation. I frequently recommend that the evaluation process include four steps.

1. *Self-evaluation.* The proactive leader is the person who has the capacity to initiate the evaluation process by developing a self-evaluation of his or her accomplishments and shortcomings during the previous year.

In many churches the process has been other-initiated rather than self-initiated. One adjudicatory developed a big, thick notebook for pastoral evaluation, inviting each pastoral committee to evaluate the pastor in each of seventeen distinct categories of ministry. At no point in the whole laborious process was the pastor invited to evaluate his or her own work performance.

This kind of other-initiated evaluation process creates reactive, passive pastors with low-grade hostility, subliminal resentment, and passive-aggressive behavior. The problem is that it does not invite the pastor to take responsibility for self-evaluation. The best way to grow forward proactive and assertive pastors is to invite them to initiate the first step in the evaluation process. That is equally important as a foundational evaluation principle for all leaders in a local church.

2. *Consultation.* The consultative step is the one in which a leader shares his or her best self-evaluation with a consultative team. The consultative team (in the case of a pastor, the pastoral

committee) then shares its best evaluation of that leader's accomplishments and shortcomings in a mutual, constructive discussion with that leader.

3. *Mutual agreement.* The leader and the consultative team develop a mutual agreement as to the central strengths and weaknesses of what has been accomplished during the past year.

4. *The coming year.* The leader and consultative team look at the coming year of the long-range plan and select the best two to four key objectives for that leader to focus on in the coming year and the best one or two specific competencies for that leader to grow forward in the coming year.

Those churches that have a strong track record of action, implementation, and momentum tend to develop excellent matches between leaders and key objectives. They have clear job descriptions that are mutually developed, including a self-initiated evaluation process that grows forward their leaders. It is not possible to teach someone to become a leader. Leaders learn to be leaders in an environment that fosters delegation of authority and self-initiated growth and development. We can't teach someone to be a leader, but a person can learn to become a leader in an environment where there is (1) an excellent match between his or her competencies and key objectives, (2) a clear job description with genuine authority, and (3) a self-initiated evaluation that focuses on improvement.

9. Motivational Resources

Churches with a strong track record of action, implementation, and momentum have an excellent match of motivational resources between key leaders, the pastor (and staff), and the grass roots in the congregation. Wherever there is a mismatch of motivational resources, there is a weak or nonexistent track record of implementation.

Motivational Resources

The five major motivational resources in churches are compassion, community, challenge, reasonability, and commitment. All five can be found in any given congregation, and usually two of the five are dominant among key leaders in that congregation. All five can be found to varying degrees in each person, and usually two of the five are dominant at a given point in that person's life pilgrimage.

All five motivational resources have equal value and weight. At a given point in a person's life pilgrimage, two of the five will usually predominate. All five are present in any given local church. Two of the five will be the prevailing motivational resources among the key leaders in that church. For there to be any sense of coherence and continuity, two of the five tend to predominate. The other three will be there in lesser ways. These five major motivational resources influence how (and whether) people give their strengths, gifts, and competencies to the work and mission of that local church.

Compassion has to do with sharing, caring, giving of one's self, and supporting. Many people do what they do in relation to a church out of the spirit of compassion. Community has to do with good fun, good times, fellowship, affiliation, belonging, and the sense of family and home. Many people do what they do in a congregation out of that sense of roots, place, and belonging. Challenge has to do with accomplishment and achievement. Some people rise to the bait of an excellent challenge.

They thrive on accomplishing things that others claim can't be done. Some people do what they do in the church out of this sense of challenge, accomplishment, and achievement.

Reasonability has to do with logic, thinking, analysis, and common sense. Some people do what they do in a church out of that sense of reasonability. Commitment has to do with dedication. Some people do what they do in a church out of a sense of faithfulness, loyalty, and dedication to that church's survival, to that church's well-being, and to that church's work and mission.

All five of these major motivational resources are present in a given congregation. Two of the five will be the predominant motivational resources among the key leaders of that congregation. Two of the five will be predominant among the grass roots. Two of the five will be predominant in the pastor (and staff). These distinctive motivational configurations constitute the motivational profile of that local church.

Motivational Matches and Mismatches

Frequently one reason some things do not happen in a local church is because what motivates the pastor differs from what motivates key leaders and the grass roots of the congregation. Sometimes the pastor and key leaders share the same motivational resources, but the grass roots has two different dominant motivational resources. They don't fit together so well. There is a "motivational gap." Please note it is not a commitment gap. Sometimes that is what pastors and key leaders mistakenly conclude, particularly if they work out of the motivational resource of commitment.

I have helped many, many churches think through the implications of the distinctive configurations of motivational resources present in their church. Imagine a church with a group of key leaders whose dominant motivational resources are challenge and commitment; grass roots members whose dominant motivational resources are compassion and community; and a pastor whose motivational resources are community and reasonability. Figure 5 helps you imagine this.

In a situation like this I frequently suggest to the key leaders, "Good friends, your *challenge* is to develop a strong *commitment* to doing what you do out of the two motivational resources of compassion and community." I suggest to the pastor, "The most

Motivational Resources

Motivators	Key Leaders	Grass Roots Members	Pastor
Compassion		x	
Community		x	x
Challenge	x		
Reasonability			x
Commitment	x		

Figure 5.   Motivational Resources in a Sample Congregation

reasonable thing you can do is to focus on the motivational resources of compassion and community."

I also share this point with both the key leaders and the pastor: "Until you bridge from your predominant motivational resources to those that are present among the grass roots, you will not motivate and mobilize the strengths, gifts, competencies, and financial resources of the grass roots." When I make these suggestions I try to bridge the motivational resources to create as helpful a match as possible.

Motivating Grass Roots Members

It happens again and again in churches—people say to me, "There are only a few of us who do everything." One reason is because those few people are working out of shared, distinctive motivational resources that match with each other but do not match with the rest of the grass roots of that congregation. Often the faithful few are motivated by commitment; the leadership recruitment is pitched toward commitment, and the grass roots members may not respond to commitment—they may respond best to compassion or community.

In thinking through how to raise funds for a fellowship hall and church school facilities, planners should design a campaign to appeal to the motivational factors of the targeted givers. Do they want to raise the money primarily from the key leaders? Do they want to raise the money primarily from the grass roots?

For example, I once asked each person on the finance committee of a church to list these five major motivational resources on a sheet of paper. I invited each of them to think about which two major motivational resources predominantly influenced the grass roots of their congregation, being careful to remind them not to think about leaders but rather the grass roots. Independently and individually, each person of the finance committee checked "compassion and community" as the major motivational resources influencing the grass roots of their church. I said to them, "The best thing you can do is to launch the fund-raising campaign with the best good-fun, good-times fellowship- and community-oriented supper this church has ever seen. And in the brochure, don't focus on the square footage of the buildings; instead show pictures of the programs that will take place in the new facilities and will advance forward person's lives and destinies in compassionate, helpful ways."

I subsequently learned that those particular key leaders were motivated primarily by challenge and commitment. But they wanted to raise the money primarily from the grass roots. The best way forward would *not* have been to launch the campaign with a Loyalty Sunday that appealed to commitment. The best way forward would *not* have been to have a "challenge goal" of some specific dollar amount that must be reached in order to do this project.

As I told that finance committee, "If you prefer to raise the money from among only the key leaders in this church, be sure to focus only on the motivational resources of challenge and commitment and you will raise the money primarily from among the key leaders." The lesson to be learned is that you need to focus on the motivational resources prevalent among the grass roots if you hope to raise the money at the grass roots level.

In stable and declining and dying churches I frequently find that many of the key leaders originally participated in the church out of the motivations of compassion and community. But over the past twenty-five years the few remaining key leaders have changed the focus of their motivation to challenge and commitment. To be sure, the only people left are those people who are committed to the challenge of trying to keep this church going so that it might minimally survive.

Sometimes I discover a church that has been badly burned by several traumatic events in recent years. In that setting the key leaders are frequently motivated by the major motivational resource of reasonability. Understandably people in this situation will hesitate—want to make sure a plan makes good sense—before they put their hand on the stove again, because the last few times they did, they got burned.

Perhaps the most overworked motivational resource in local churches is commitment. When someone says to me, "What we need in our church is more commitment," my response is, "You have just taught me that a major motivational resource out of which you do what you do in the church is commitment. But, good friend, there are other persons who come to church—who do what they do in the church—out of a sense of compassion, community, challenge, or reasonability."

Frequently key leaders and pastors whose primary motivational resource is commitment press the congregation to remember their membership vows. If you are a person for whom compassion is a primary motivational resource, the phrase "remember your membership vows" may end up sounding like "remember to clean up your room." To be sure, the membership vows of many denominations were written by people whose primary motivation was commitment. In some churches it would make better sense during the financial campaign to have compassion cards rather than commitment cards. In some churches it would make better sense to have a Love Sunday rather than a Loyalty Sunday. In some churches it would make better sense to have a Community Sunday rather than a Commitment Sunday.

Competencies and Commitment

It is not true that all ministers are incompetent. It is not even true that only some ministers are incompetent. It is true that some people are incompetent as ministers. That does not mean they are incompetent; it means simply that they are incompetent only for the position of minister. It is not true that shortstops are incompetent. It is true that some people who are competent as shortstops are incompetent as pitchers. Some persons do not have the competencies for some positions. They do have the competencies for other positions.

Some people who are incompetent as ministers use the bludgeon of commitment to excuse their own ineptness. As a matter of fact, the ploy of charging people with lack of commitment is often an effort at guilt transference. Some people are aware of their own ineptness and incompetence but try to transfer guilt to the members by using the push for commitment. When things don't go well, they blame the grass roots for a lack of commitment when, in fact, the problem is their lack of competencies. Sometimes a declining worship attendance is due to the lack of a preaching competency. Some few ministers, rather than working on their preaching, will fall back on blaming the grass roots for a lack of commitment. Frankly, preaching—however inept—which focuses on the motivational resources of compassion and community will go further than preaching which pulverizes people for their lack of commitment.

It is regrettable that commitment has become the most overworked motivational resource in many churches. Further, it is regrettable that inept, incompetent persons use the excuse of lack of commitment as their way to divert responsibility.

Compassion and Community

Many, many unchurched persons are attracted to churches that communicate and share a sense of compassion and community rather than a sense of commitment. Commitment is a motivational resource developed among "mature Christians." But what draws and attracts people to a church is their search for a sense of sharing and caring in which they can participate. What draws people to a church is their search for community—roots, place, belonging. People are frequently drawn to a church by the two major motivational resources of compassion and community.

For example, one new congregation mails out a brochure in its area. The cover of the brochure reads, "Join in the challenge of starting a new   (denominational name)   church." Such a brochure focuses on and appeals to people motivated by challenge—high achievement and accomplishment-oriented people—who are already a part of that denomination. The brochure for another new church has on the front a line drawing of a church and of a home. The only words on the front of the brochure are, "Your friend next door." It is an appeal to compassion and to community.

One reason some of the mainline Protestant denominations in the country are experiencing decline is because their focus is principally on the motivational resource of commitment—which is somewhat like a focus on the "advanced trigonometry" of church membership—when in fact many, many people seek out churches that focus on the "basic math" of compassion and community.

It is helpful to do a thoughtful analysis of the predominant motivational resources operative in your congregration. It is not as simplistic as focusing only on commitment. In one area of the United States dominated by high-tech industry, a particular church's key leaders have the two dominant motivational resources of challenge and reasonability—they are scientists and engineers, growing entrepreneurs in electronics. The grass roots of that congregation is an excellent match in terms of challenge and reasonability, and the church has a strong track record of action, implementation, and momentum because of that excellent match. This can occur in a locale where the two predominant motivational resources are prevalent in the community as well as the church. And indeed a large number of people in that area share the same two major motivational resources—namely, challenge and reasonability. So it is an excellent match across the board.

I find this analysis of motivational resources most intriguing and most helpful. To be sure, I have developed this material out of my own research and reflections. At the same time, on each occasion I share this with groups and give them the chance to compare the motivational resources among key leaders, grass roots, pastor, and the unchurched, it becomes increasingly self-apparent to them why some churches have a strong track record of action, implementation, and momentum and some do not.

As a leader in your church you should be aware of and sensitive to ways of nurturing forward a match of the motivational resources present among leaders, pastor, and grass roots. You will want to analyze these motivational resources for your church. Check your best judgment on figure 6. The closer the match, the higher the probability of a strong track record of action, implementation, and momentum. The more bridging of differences that can be achieved, the more likely the momentum.

Motivational Resources

Motivators	Key Leaders	Grass Roots Members	Pastor	Unchurched
Compassion				
Community				
Challenge				
Reasonability				
Commitment				

Figure 6.   Motivational Resources in Your Congregation

10. Leadership Development: Focusing on the Middle Third

Leaders do not grow on trees. You cannot go out and pick a new crop of leaders each fall. Qualities of leadership must be developed and enhanced among your current leaders. Qualities of leadership must be nurtured forward among the grass roots. As new people join your church you must look for ways to nurture their leadership contribution to the life and mission of your church. But you have a limited amount of time and energy to invest in developing leadership competencies. Where will you focus your efforts?

Churches with a strong track record of action, implementation, and momentum invest the majority of their leadership development effort on the middle third of their leaders. Whenever the major emphasis of leadership development is elsewhere, that church will not nurture forward a rich range of new, competent leaders.

Stages of Development

Any group of people can be divided into thirds—a first third, a middle third, and a third third—in relation to the stage of development of each individual's leadership competencies. I recognize that some persons would suggest the following designations: top third, middle third, and bottom third. I am reluctant to use the terms *top* and *bottom;* they suggest a more hierarchical order than makes sense to me. I recognize that the term *third third* is awkward, but I prefer it over the alternative. *Bottom* and *top* suggest a more permanent situation, when, in fact, these groups constitute stages of leadership development.

The first third includes persons whose leadership competencies are an 8, 9, or 10 on a scale of 1 to 10. The first third frequently is composed of persons who have been in leadership situations a long time and have had considerable leadership experience. They may function in a leadership role in their everyday work life. They are comfortable in the role of leader and move forward to complete leadership projects set before them.

The middle third includes persons whose leadership competencies, for the present, are a 5, 6, or 7 on a scale of 1 to 10. The middle third frequently is composed of people who feel comfortable in some leadership situations but whose competencies can be advanced. These people have the potential for further growth and development of their leadership competencies into the first third.

The third third are persons whose leadership competencies, for the present, are a 1 to 4 on a scale of 1 to 10. This third frequently is composed of people whose current competencies are more as followers than leaders. Such people play an important supporting role in the leadership of the church. But don't invest your major resources of time and energy trying to force their leadership competencies from a rating of 1 to 4 to a rating of 8 or 9. Give them excellent supporting jobs, which they have genuine competencies to accomplish, and then affirm the value of what they achieve. They will advance their leadership skills, though perhaps their pace will be more measured than some others. Help them to grow their leadership competencies from 1 to 4 to 5, 6, or 7, not 8, 9, or 10.

Four Mistakes

Some may be surprised that I would suggest that a realistic assessment of leadership competencies is important. Some churches have a poor track record of action, implementation, and momentum precisely because they are naïve and idealistic about leadership competencies. These churches commmit four grievous mistakes. First, they assume some people are leaders and some are followers. Second, they assume leaders have essentially the same leadership competencies. Third, they assume any leader can be plugged into any leadership role—so long as he or she is willing. Fourth, they assume that if someone is given a job, he or she will therefore become a leader.

1. It is too simplistic to divide people into two categories, leaders and followers. Regrettably a few pastors and key leaders have said to me that they categorize people into two classes,

winners and losers. Fortunately few people hold that extreme view. But I reject even the milder position that some people are leaders and some are followers. At certain times each of us serves as a leader and at other times each serves as a follower. The roles interchange based on the occasion, the group of people involved, and the specific competencies called for at that time. Virtually every person has served both as leader and as follower. These are dynamic, developmental roles and people cannot be classified permanently in either one.

2. There is a diversity of strengths and competencies. As we saw in chapter 6 there is a range of complementary strengths and competencies. Virtually all people have each of the following strengths to some degree: leading and caring, supporting and giving, analytical and diagnostic, and social and relational strengths.

All four are present, and at the same time one of the four is likely to be the most developed and predominant competency within an individual at a given point in his or her life's pilgrimage. In a particular setting, with a specific group, that distinctive competency will be decisive, and under those conditions that individual will serve as leader. When analytical and diagnostic competencies are needed the person who has developed that competency will serve as leader. Furthermore, the diversity of gifts is broader than even these four strengths—therefore, people cannot be classified simply as leaders or followers.

The assumption that leaders have essentially the same leadership competencies is foolish. We have already seen that there is a diversity of gifts. For each individual leader each of his or her strengths will be at a distinctive stage of development. A realistic assessment of leadership development affirms that there are several stages of development for each strength.

You can use figure 7 to plot your own current leadership competencies. On the bar graph for each set of strengths, draw a line where you estimate your own competency to be, and shade in the bar graph below this line. For those strengths where you estimate your competency to be at the level of 8, 9, or 10, you are in the first third stage of leadership development. For those strengths where you estimate your competency to be at the level of 5, 6, or 7, you are in the middle third stage of leadership development. And for those gifts where you estimate your com-

Your Leadership Competencies

Stage of Development	Strengths			
	Leading and Caring	Supporting and Giving	Analytical and Diagnostic	Social and Relational
10[a]				
9				
8				
7				
6				
5				
4				
3				
2				
1				

[a]On a scale of 1 to 10, with 10 being the greatest level of development

Figure 7. An Analysis of Your Own Leadership Competencies

petency to be at the level of 1, 2, 3, or 4, you are in the third third stage of leadership development.

Life is a pilgrimage and we grow and develop in distinctive ways. And no person is locked into the position of being a third third. People grow forward their distinctive competencies in developmental, dynamic ways.

3. It is simply not the case that any current leader can be plugged into any leadership role. As we have seen, there *is* a

diversity of gifts. Some churches tend to commit this third mistake as they scramble to fill the empty slots they have in their organizational and committee structure. Study samples of the leadership surveys and time and talent surveys used in many churches. Most are primarily designed to find people to fill the church's needs. But churches with a strong record of action, implementation, and momentum focus on helping individuals to discover where they can best fulfill their competencies, not where they can fill some slot.

4. It is a mistake to assume that if you give someone a job he or she will become a leader. Some churches are particularly prone to do this with new members. They assume that giving the new member a job will help him or her to become a leader. When the new member is given the wrong job—that is, a poor match is made—you are on your way to creating an inactive member. People do learn to be leaders—they cannot be taught to be leaders, but they can learn leadership. And they learn it best when there is an excellent match between their leadership competencies and the key objectives of the post in which they serve.

Regrettably some churches do not exercise care and thought as to an excellent match. Because of this mistake some churches create third third leaders—that is, the person is functioning with a leadership strength of 1 to 4 because of a poor match. But were the person in a post that constituted an excellent match, his or her leadership contribution might be an 8, 9, or 10. You and your church should develop a realistic assessment of the leadership competencies present in your church.

A Wise Investment

For illustrative purposes assume that in a given group of congregational leaders there are thirty persons with a range of leadership competencies. Ten of the thirty leaders might be in the first third, ten might be in the middle third, and ten might be in the third third. (In practice the breakdown does not always fall into even thirds.) The mistake many churches make is in investing their major leadership development time and effort with the third third. Often they invest 15 percent of their leadership development efforts with the first third, 25 percent with the middle third, and 60 percent with the third third.

Table 5.   The Division of Time Spent Developing Leaders and the Likely Result

Method 1.   Many Churches Do This

Competency Level	Leaders Now at This Level	Time Spent with These Leaders	Leaders Likely to Be at This Level in 3 Years
First third	10	15%	10
Middle third	10	25%	10
Third third	10	**60%**	10

Method 2.   A Better Way to Develop Leaders

Competency Level	Leaders Now at This Level	Time Spent with These Leaders	Leaders Likely to Be at This Level in 3 Years
First third	10	15%	16
Middle third	10	60%	6
Third third	10	25%	8

The art of growing forward the total leadership team is to swap the leadership development time investment between the middle and third third, so that your church is now spending 60 percent of its time on the middle third and 25 percent of its time on the third third. This is a wise investment of your leadership development time. Table 5 illustrates this principle and its effectiveness.

Please note that I am describing only leadership development time. You may invest 60 percent of your missional care time, your pastoral care time, your shepherding time with the third

third. But invest 60 percent of your leadership development time with the middle third if you want to grow your leadership resources forward. No one should use the leadership development principle of the middle third as an excuse to neglect missional, pastoral, and shepherding responsibilities. Indeed, developing leadership among the middle third will deliver a richer, fuller range of leadership resources with which to advance the sharing of missional, pastoral, and shepherding care.

The art is to grow forward the leadership competencies of at least six out of the ten middle-third leaders to excellent first-third leaders. This accomplishes two important objectives. First, leadership shifts strongly to assertive, intentional, highly creative leaders. You have a leadership team in which sixteen out of the thirty persons are now rated in the first third. The number of excellent leaders in relation to the team as a whole has been increased considerably by growing forward these six persons.

Second, the standard of excellence for leadership is markedly advanced. The higher the standard of excellence for the team as a whole, the more likely are third-third leaders to grow forward. Conversely, when leadership strengths merely maintain the status quo, third-third leaders are more likely to continue in the third third. Advancing the standard of excellence provides major encouragement for all leaders.

More Help Than Would Be Helpful

Some people are attracted to investing 60 percent of their time with third-third leaders because they genuinely want to be helpful. Sometimes they also want to create people who are dependent upon them. They imagine that by focusing on third-third leaders they are somehow conserving and protecting these people. As a matter of fact, they are delivering coddling, not caring. They are sharing more help than would be helpful. Their help is harmful. They create dependent persons, not leaders.

The parable of the good steward is a helpful text for leadership development. The good steward, when given five talents, developed five more. The good steward, when given two talents, developed two more. The steward who was given one talent and buried it in the ground was the one cast into outer darkness. His master said to him, "You didn't even invest it so that it would earn interest." Good stewardship of our leadership gifts and competencies implies advancing and developing them. Good stewardship is not conserving and preserving these gifts as they are.

For example, a church school superintendent may frequently focus 60 percent or more of his or her time primarily with that third third of the church school teachers who seem to be having the most difficulty. But three years from now they will still be having the most difficulty. And three years from now the quality and character of the church school as a whole will be essentially the same. Similarly chairpersons of committees frequently make the mistake of investing 60 percent of their leadership time with the third third of the people on the committee who are not delivering the work. Three years from now the achievements of the committee will have changed little. Some key leaders and pastors make the mistake of spending the majority of their leadership development time with people who are virtually inactive in the life of that church. Three years later the church will be essentially the same as before.

Years ago, while working with people who struggle with alcoholism, I learned that when people in helping roles allow themselves to be controlled by the people they are trying to help, they only prove that they are not really in the helping role at all. I have met myself coming and going in situations when someone who could not control his own behavior ran me around the mulberry bush. And when someone like an alcoholic, who cannot control his own behavior, manages to control the behavior of the helping person, it becomes clear to the alcoholic that the helping person is not a source of real help at all. Innately the alcoholic senses that what he or she needs is a helping person who can control his or her behavior and model and parallel how life can be lived with a reasonable amount of control.

People in helping roles allow themselves to be controlled primarily because they are intent on sharing help, but they end up delivering more help than would be helpful. Now, I am not comparing third-third leaders and alcoholics. I am comparing what helping persons tend to do both with third-third leaders and alcoholics. They deliver more help than would be helpful.

The mistake many persons make in leadership development is that they share more help than is helpful. The art is to share just enough help to be helpful, and no more.

"Grassfires" and Dependency

Churches and key leaders too frequently invest 60 percent of their leadership development time with the third third because they are interested in being helpful. The third-third leader, for lack of leadership competency, often starts a "grassfire," and other leaders, out of their own anxiety and desire to be helpful, come running to help put out the grassfire. They deliver recognition, attention, affection, and concern. They teach the person that one of the best things he or she can do to get attention is start another grassfire. People will go running to help put it out again. They will deliver recognition, attention, affection, and concern. And a cycle of grassfires and people who come running to put them out is created.

I distinguish between a grassfire and a forest fire. But when in doubt give the third-third leader the chance to learn from his or her mistakes rather than protecting him or her from failure. One of the best friends and teachers an alcoholic has is pain. When all of the pain is quickly relieved, the person struggling with alcoholism no longer has available to him or her that excellent good friend and teacher. And when someone runs to help a third-third leader put out a grassfire, that helper removes one of the most constructive friends and teachers the leader has available—namely, the pain associated with learning from one's own mistakes.

As a child my wife, Julie, played with someone who set off fireworks in a vacant lot and started a real grassfire. People nearby pitched in to put it out—even the fire department was called to help put it out. Once the damage had been contained, the child's aunt had a firm discussion with her to be sure that she understood what she had done, how much fright it had caused the neighbors (fortunately in this case no serious property damage occurred), what might have happened, and what behavior was expected—indeed, counted on—in the future.

When a "grassfire" happens in a church, people rush to help, wanting to minimize the damage. But all too often the person responsible gets an overdose of supportive concern and forgiveness and an underdose of accountability. The supervisor of the person who started the "fire" needs to sit down with him or her and have a firm discussion to help him or her learn from the event—to make sure the person understands what he or she has done (or not done), what has (or hasn't) happened, what might have happened, and what behavior is counted on in the future.

You don't want to teach people a pattern of starting grassfires, confident that other leaders will come running to help put them out. That phenomenon of investing 60 percent of a group's time and resources with the third third of our leaders creates passive, dependent followers, because other people come running to deliver recognition, attention, affection, and concern.

I propose that 25 percent of your church's leadership development time be directed toward advancing the strengths and competencies of third-third leaders. The art is to work with persons whose leadership competencies are in the range of 1 to 4 and help them grow their competencies forward to a range of 5 to 7. Do not set the unrealistic objective of growing each of them forward to an 8, 9, or 10 immediately. Let them set the pace and help them keep moving forward.

Let me reiterate this point. I am *not* suggesting that third-third leaders be ignored. In all of my coaching I have followed the policy that whoever shows up for practice plays. Mostly you go with the team you have and coach them forward. But the danger of investing 60 percent of one's leadership development time (as distinguished from one's shepherding time) with the third third is that one creates a pattern of dependency and passivity, because the person learns that when he or she starts a "grassfire" someone will come running to put it out. All too frequently the person who comes running "needs" to have people dependent on him or her, and that parasitic relationship does not create leaders but keeps people dependent.

The way forward is to invest 60 percent of your leadership development time with the middle third. Match extraordinarily well the key objectives with middle-third leaders, help them to develop an excellent job description and a self-initiated evaluation process, and put them in the stance of growing themselves forward in proactive and assertive ways. This investment of leadership development helps the middle third, the third third, and the first third. Three years from now the character and quality of the leadership team of a given church will thereby be substantially advanced. And such a church will have a strong track record of action, implementation, and momentum.

11. Excellent Mistakes and Objectives Worth Not Doing

An interesting phenomenon I have observed in churches with a strong track record of action, implementation, and momentum is the valuing and honoring of excellent mistakes. These churches have developed a corporate value for appreciating, recognizing, and rewarding lessons learned from excellent mistakes. There is a direct correlation between excellent mistakes and the level of creativity and productivity in a church. The more a church appreciates, recognizes, and rewards excellent mistakes, the more that group nurtures forward the level of creativity and productivity in the organization. The organization that is not making mistakes is the organization that is not doing anything.

Some years ago when I first took up sailing I was concerned about the possibility that we might run aground—that the sailboat's deep keel would lodge on a sandbar or reef. As we talked with other sailors it soon became clear that the old saying was true: The skipper who says that he has never run aground is the skipper who has never left the dock. You are bound to run aground sometime. You are also likely to make mistakes. Some churches become so anxious and fearful about making mistakes that they never "leave the dock."

Rather than focus on avoiding mistakes, focus on moving ahead. Build and nurture the understanding that some mistakes will happen. We don't want them to happen and we will do our level best to avoid them. But if we make a mistake we will learn from it, and we will not make the same mistake again.

The baseball player does not get a hit each time at bat, but he or she hopes to. Often a player flies out or strikes out. Sometimes he or she is thrown out at first. It doesn't work to expect a home run each time at bat. However, very few baseball players get anywhere by trying to avoid striking out or by never stepping up to the plate. We need to do as these players do—go to the plate with a relaxed intentionality to do well on this pitch and to learn from any excellent mistakes we make.

I am not suggesting that valuing lessons learned from excellent mistakes can be misconstrued as an excuse for condoning mistakes. Some churches adopt a "poor little me" attitude, thinking they can never do anything right. They expect that their chances of doing anything right are slim. Sure enough it becomes a self-fulfilling prophecy: They never do anything right. They do not even achieve a mediocre middle. Rather, I am describing the quality of church that values excellent, solid, creative, risk-taking mistakes. Those mistakes are costly. And in creative, constructive ways we learn substantially and beneficially from these mistakes.

For years I have been convinced of the principle that people lead in direct relation to the way they experience being led. Recently I was teaching at the seminary of a denomination in which there is a theological perspective that encourages a kind of compulsiveness toward perfectionism. In many respects the ministers of that denomination are encouraged never to make a mistake. Indeed, it is the practice that mistakes they make are noted on their personnel record, which follows them for most of their ministerial life.

I was meeting with the faculty of that seminary at their annual retreat, serving as their resource leader and consultant. We were discussing that specific dilemma and the faculty members' observation that it creates ministers who are tense, tight, fearful, cautious, nonrisking—who do what is minimally expected of them in passive, reactive ways. There is not a great deal of creativity, there is not a great deal of action, and there is not a great deal of accomplishment and achievement.

People lead in direct relation to the way they experience being led. At the retreat we talked about the idea that people teach in direct relation to the way they experience being taught. People minister in direct relation to the way in which they experience being ministered to. So I proposed to that faculty that they have a good year of teaching and that in the spring they have the fun of discussing and thinking through together who among the faculty had learned the most from making the "best mistake of the year." I also suggested that part of the honors program on graduation day be the presentation to the faculty member who had successfully made the best mistake of the year. I suggested to them that one of the important things they could share with their students is the ability to learn from the best mistake of the year. This would show the graduating ministers in that denomination that excellent mistakes are appreciated, valued, and rewarded. People lead in direct relation to the way they experience being led.

I have been in churches where someone twenty-five years before said that that church was doomed. Yes, there are fewer people and they all have graying hair, but that church has hung on and clung to a bare, meager existence for over a quarter of a century. The problem that began to develop was the fear of doing anything out of the fear of failure. Particularly in stable and declining and dying churches there is a sense in which people freeze, become immobilized, afraid to do anything for fear they might do something wrong.

One of the healthiest things we can do is to understand that churches are tough, resilient, long-lasting creations of God. The art is to creatively and constructively move forward, understanding that some of the key objectives we may have included in our long-range plan will be excellent mistakes.

In their book *In Search of Excellence* Waterman and Peters have identified a bias for action as a common thread among America's best-run companies. Our churches, too, need that bias for action. Indeed, if the choice has to be made, the church is better off to choose slightly uncoordinated action over fully coordinated inaction. The premium placed on coordination in many of the major denominations is precisely one of the reasons those denominations are in trouble. It is as though they must coordinate everything neatly and tidily so as to ensure that everyone is together and no mistake will ever be made.

We need more creativity and less coordination. We need more action, accomplishment, and achievement and fewer meetings and less coordination. Central to that bias for action is nurturing forward the corporate value of excellent mistakes, which enhance creativity, productivity, action, implementation, and momentum.

Objectives Worth Not Doing

Churches with a strong track record for action, implementation, and momentum know that some objectives are worth not doing. In even the most effective long-range plans there may be two or three key objectives that turn out to be excellent mistakes. It is equally true that even in the best long-range plans there may turn out to be one or two key objectives that are worth not doing.

Sometimes we don't work on some key objectives because we sense the failure implicit in them. Most persons and most groups gravitate toward success, not failure. Sometimes, when we closely analyze why a church has not accomplished some of its key objectives, we discover that those key objectives may very well have set up that church to fail, not succeed. Some key objectives may appear to be excellent in the early stages of developing an effective long-range plan. But as the planning team puts the plan into place and the dynamic of momentum begins to build, it becomes clear that they were wrong—one or two key objectives are worth not doing.

There is a difference between valuing excellent mistakes and recognizing that an objective is not worth doing. In a church that values excellent mistakes some person, task force, or committee tries to accomplish a key objective and in the process achieves an excellent mistake. But deciding that an objective is not worth doing has more to do with those key objectives that no one works on.

Even in the very best long-range plans there will be one or two key objectives that fall by the wayside—no one takes up the banner to lead them forward. Why does that happen? Sometimes it is because none of the people on the leadership team senses a good match with that key objective. Sometimes it is because the motivational resources related to that objective do not match with the motivational resources of key leaders and the grass roots of the congregation. And sometimes it is because people sense innately that the objective is of lesser priority than other objectives on the list. Sometimes nothing happens because people sense that that objective is a setup for failure, not success.

Having the value that some objectives are worth not doing helps people to be more realistic in evaluating the past and revising plans for the coming years of the long-range plan, including adding the new year. Too many churches discover several objectives they intended to accomplish but have not achieved and begin to berate themselves for lack of commitment. They have now become slaves of their own plan. The plan is dominating their perspective and perception. The plan is always the creature of those who have participated in creating it.

With this value strongly in place as part of our corporate self-understanding, we can let some objectives go, forget them, and understand that in the end they were not worth doing. This decision is reached in light of the objectives we are accomplishing and in the light of those objectives that for us have become excellent mistakes and from which we have learned in constructive, creative ways. Some churches cling to an objective created four years before simply because it was created four years before and they feel they should do something with it. Finally, some objectives are worth letting go and not doing. Churches that have a strong track record of action, implementation, and momentum have nurtured forward both the value of excellent mistakes and the value that some objectives are finally worth not doing.

12. Prayer: Vision and Hope

Churches with a strong track record of action, implementation, and momentum have developed a prayer life that has about it the qualities of vision and hope. Planning and prayer go together.

The invitational questions shared in chapter 4 will help to focus your church's prayer life. In helping your congregation to focus its prayer life for planning, your church should hold before itself these invitational questions:

Where are we headed?
What kind of future are we building?
What are our strengths, gifts, and competencies?
What is God calling us to accomplish in mission?

These invitational questions are particularly appropriate focal points for the prayer life of your congregation as it shares in developing an effective long-range plan.

You are not praying for precise, definitive, once-for-all-time answers to these invitational questions. Rather, the spirit of your prayer life together is rooted in asking for God's guidance as you pray and puzzle through where you are headed, the kind of future you are building, the strengths, gifts and competencies you have, and the mission you plan to accomplish in response to God's calling. Frequently these invitational questions are shared richly and fully with the congregation. Much is at stake in the development of an effective long-range plan. And since much is at stake, we are called to pray with the wisdom, judgment, vision, and common sense that comes to us as gifts from God.

Who We Pray For

During the development of an effective long-range plan, the congregation should be invited to share in prayer on behalf of your mutual work to develop an effective long-range plan. The congregation should be invited to pray with and for the key leaders facilitating the development of the church's long-range plan. The congregation should pray that these key leaders will guide you through the four stages of effective long-range planning and that, as a result of focusing on these four stages, an effective long-range plan will emerge for the coming three, five, or seven years in the life of your congregation. Encourage the grass roots members of the congregation to pray that their own excellent ideas, good suggestions, thoughtful judgments, and realistic visions will contribute creatively and constructively to fashioning the future for this congregation.

Further, encourage the congregation to pray for the pastor and the staff so that their shepherding, caring, insights, compassion, and competencies will be particularly present in "this time." Finally, encourage the congregation to pray for the people this congregation hopes to help in mission—people who will enrich the congregation in return as they are helped with their own lives and destinies.

In response to the question, "Who is my neighbor?" Jesus told the parable of the Good Samaritan. One interesting interpretation of that parable is that the neighbor is the man in the ditch. That interpretation affirms that it is the good neighbor who calls forth the best in the other. The man in the ditch called forth the best in the Samaritan who, in the centuries that have come and gone since, has been called the Good Samaritan.

This is not intended in a paternalistic way. Rather, it affirms that when we seek to help with specific human hurts and hopes, it is truly a mutual process—and sometimes it is finally hard to determine who has helped whom the most. And it is important that our prayer life during this time of planning and expectancy include looking forward to helping and to being helped by people whom we have not yet had the privilege of meeting.

Praying Without Ceasing

The number of churches that do not pray as part of long-range planning amazes me. It is particularly important and appropriate that each planning session begin and conclude with prayer—prayer that is not full of abstract generalities and vague, ambiguous concerns. But each time of prayer should richly and deeply invite the full, stirring presence of God, who dwells with us and among us as we plan on behalf of his cause.

Indeed, you can invite the whole congregation to be in an attitude, spirit, and time of prayer during the weeks or months in which its long-range plan is being developed. Further, it is most helpful to invite a specific group of people to have the privilege and task of praying for your work together as you seek to discover and discern the future in mission that God has both promised and prepared for your church.

I recall a church in which a vibrant, caring, men's prayer breakfast group took upon itself the rich, full task of praying for the congregation, for the key leaders, for the pastor, for the staff, and for the countless people this church would touch in years to come as the church engaged in developing its long-range plan. I recall another church where it was the Wednesday night Bible study group that shared this task and privilege. In yet another church it was one of the women's circles that contributed to the prayer life of the planning venture. It is important that some group be invited to carry forward this sense of prayer in the midst of planning.

The practice of praying should really be a standard way of life in a local church. Instead, we often ask leaders to take a job and then we never pray for or with them during the year in which they have that post. In many churches there is a time of praying with and for the Sunday School teachers before their classes, a time of praying with and for the chairpersons and the committees substantively engaged in the administrative and de-cision-making life of the church, and a time of praying with and for the mission teams, the visitation teams, the choir, significant relational groups—all those people and groups that have dis-tinctive leadership roles in the life of the church.

Vision and Hope

Those churches that have a strong track record of action, im-plementation, and momentum actively practice their prayer life in the midst of their planning, and that practice of prayer life distinctively includes the qualities of vision and hope.

I have been in church after church where the Sunday morning bulletins share the names of the sick and dying. And during the time of prayer concerns people speak out to say for whom they would like to pray. Inevitably those prayer concerns focus on the sick and dying. This teaches every person gathered there, including every first-time visitor, that this is primarily a sick and dying church.

I was with one church at a special Sunday morning service of remembrance. Printed in the church bulletin were the names of every person who had died during the previous year. At the appropriate time in the service the pastor read each name slowly. The church bell tolled in the background and the organ was gently played. A helpful prayer of triumph followed and then was sung a strong hymn of celebration for the dead, for who they had been with us, for who they are with us, and for who they are with God. It was a moving, meaningful service.

After the service the pastor asked me what I thought. I told him the service was most helpful. And then I said to him, "When do you do the same service for those people who have been born this past year? When do you do the same for those people who are celebrating major accomplishment and achievement in their own lives?"

We want the help of prayers when we are ill or dying. But life is not a matter of sickness and death only. Life is also a matter of vision and hope. During the development of an effective long-range plan our prayer life should take seriously those occasions of vision and hope as well as those tragic, traumatic events in which we experience illness and death. God is with us at all times.

When do you have your service of worship? Recently I have come to understand that stable and growing churches tend to celebrate their service of worship on the first day of the week; that is, the pastor, the choir director, the worship leaders, the ushers, the greeters of newcomers, and the key leaders in the church understand that this service of worship begins the week. Whenever I find this spirit, I tend to find a well-prepared service of worship. It has the qualities of integrity and spontaneity, of vision and hope. I tend to find a service that launches the week to come with expectancy and a sense of excitement.

In contrast, whenever I find a stable and declining church, I tend to find a church where worship is seen as happening on the last day of the week, not the first. It seems that whenever pastors and key leaders think of worship as occurring on the last day of the week, two things happen. Worship becomes less well prepared; it is what is left over, the last thing done in the week. And the worship service tends to look back on what has been; it tends to summarize the week that was rather than look forward to the week that will be. There are really only two things we can do with the week that has been: we can ask God's forgiveness for our sins and shortcomings, and we can thank God for those gifts and strengths with which he has blessed us this past week. But we cannot change what has been.

As you develop your long-range plan, plan to celebrate worship on the first day of the week. If you think your week begins on Monday morning in the office or at your job, your worship is occurring on the last day of the week. Some pastors make the mistake of thinking their work week begins on Monday morning in the office rather than on Sunday in worship with the congregation. Whenever a pastor sees his or her work week beginning with worship on the first day of the week, there will be a sense of expectancy, vision, and hope in that church.

We are not a people of the cross only. And those churches that become preoccupied with the cross only—and think of themselves as sick and dying only—know only a portion of the gospel. Yes, life is sickness and death. But there is more to the good news than simply the cross. There is a description of a group of people who walked to a tomb on the first day of the week. We are a first-day people. We are the Easter people. We are the people of the open tomb, the risen Lord, and new life in Christ. We are the people of vision and hope.

Churches that nurture the practice of their prayer life during the development of their long-range plan create effective long-range plans. And those churches have a high track record of action, implementation, and momentum. This is decisively true when their prayer life has about it the qualities of vision and hope.

Now, as leaders in the development of an effective long-range plan, I invite you to think through which of the seven qualities discussed in part 2 are already well in place in your church. Of those qualities that are already well in place, which ones can you nurture forward even more fully? Of those qualities among the seven not now well in place, which ones can you grow, build, and enhance as you move through the development of an effective long-range plan? The more fully these qualities are well in place, the higher the probability that your church will have a strong track record of action, implementation, and momentum.

Part Three
FOUR DYNAMICS TO CONSIDER

13. Memory, Change, Conflict, and Hope

Hope is stronger than memory. Memory is strong; hope is stronger. Four dynamics contribute to any present moment in the life and work of a local church. Indeed, these four dynamics contribute to any present and future moment in the life and work of that congregation. The four dynamics are memory, change, conflict, and hope. Their relationship is illustrated by figure 8 and is examined in this chapter.

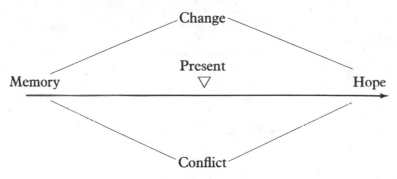

Figure 8.   Four Dynamics Affecting the Present

From one local church to another these four dynamics live themselves out in distinct ways. As leaders of your church it will be most helpful for you to be sensitive to the unique and distinctive ways these four dynamics are influencing the present understandings and perceptions in your local church. Further, as leaders you should assist the congregation in being aware of the ways in which distinctive events of memory, change, conflict, and hope have contributed and will contribute to the shaping of the perceptions and perspectives present in the congregation.

Memory

Memory is strong because memory is about those past events that decisively contribute to our present understandings and perceptions. We remember five kinds of events that contribute to our perceptions. We remember tragic events that mar and scar our lives; these memories profoundly affect our sense of the future as well as the past. We remember sinful events in which we have participated, and we ask God's forgiveness and the forgiveness of others for our participation in those sinful events. We remember incidental events; we don't know quite why we remember them, but they are present with us and shape our current perceptions. We also remember celebrative events—birthdays, anniversaries, events in which we celebrate accomplishments and achievements.

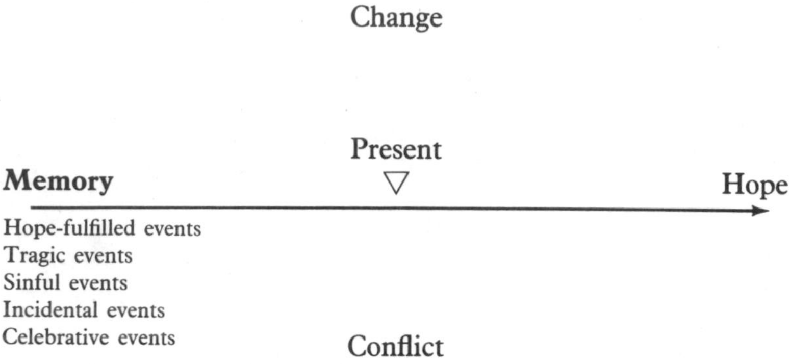

Change

Present

Memory   ▽   Hope

Hope-fulfilled events
Tragic events
Sinful events
Incidental events
Celebrative events   Conflict

Figure 9.   The Dynamic of Memory

But most important, we remember hope-fulfilled events. We remember those events in which our deepest longings, yearnings, and hopes were decisively fulfilled. Some people make the mistake of assuming that congregations are primarily creatures of custom, habit, and tradition. To be sure, congregations develop richly and fully a wide range of unique customs, habits, and traditions. But if one looks closely at the traditions present in a church, one discovers that the most powerful traditions are not about events of memory in an historical sense of the past. The most powerful, profound traditions churches celebrate recall those events in which the congregation's own hopes for the future were most dramatically and decisively fulfilled. One church I know of had some of its deepest longings, yearnings, and hopes decisively fulfilled in an event in 1886. And what they did in 1887, 1888, 1889, and every year since has developed the tradition of honoring that future-based, hope-fulfilled event.

One reason memory is strong is that memory is about hope. It is in memory that people remember those events of hope. That is what Passover is about. That is what the Exodus is about. That is what the open tomb and risen Lord and new life in Christ are about. These are not events of the past. These are events in which the future—the future of our hopes—has been decisively fulfilled.

I invite you as leaders to be sensitive to and to think through the dynamic of memory as it distinctively lives itself out in your congregation. I invite you to be thinking of the several events of memory that are distinctive and decisive for your church. With a sense of wisdom and judgment think through those events, whether tragic, sinful, incidental, celebrative, or hope-fulfilled, that inform and shape the present moment and your congregation's perceptions of the future.

Change

Two kinds of change have forceful impact upon a congregation. Most churches are sensitive to external changes that have affected them and will continue to affect them in the future. Such external changes range from the establishment of a strong, dynamic new congregation half a mile away, which now vibrantly contributes nine out of the twelve central characteristics, to the building of a six-lane highway that has shaped in fresh new ways the traffic direction patterns of a community or to the opening or closing of a factory. There are economic, social, political, vocational, recreational, religious, demographic, and geographic sources of external change that have strong impact on a local church. As leaders you should think through and be sensitive to the distinctive external sources of change that affect your local congregation.

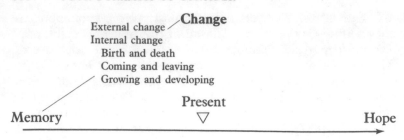

Present
▽
Memory   Hope

Conflict

Figure 10. The Dynamic of Change

Most important, think through the internal sources of change that decisively contribute to the dynamics of your congregation. Regrettably churches become preoccupied with the external sources of change. Equally important, and sometimes more important, are the internal sources of change that contribute substantially and significantly to a church's character. One internal source of change is that some persons are born and some persons die in a congregation. For example, at Pleasant Valley Church, which was anything but pleasant some of the time, Lois was the linking person in a two-cell congregation. Pleasant Valley was richly and fully a two-cell congregation and two-cell congregations do one thing extraordinarily well—they fight. This was a fight between the old-timers and the newcomers, the pioneers and the homesteaders, the cattlemen and the sheepherders. And the fight was on.

At Pleasant Valley, Lois, the daughter of the patriarch of the old-timers, was married to one of the newcomers. She provided a constructive, although tenuous, link that minimized the intensity of the fighting. Late one Saturday evening, coming back from a teachers' meeting in the heavy rains of that fall, a semi-tractor-trailer smashed to smithereens the car in which Lois and five other teachers rode. And the link between the two cells was no more. And that church was now a two-cell church with all the richness of a two-cell church, plus the anger and fury over the loss of the favorite daughter; the hope for the future was dead. That sense of anger and fury and terror compounded an already difficult two-cell church fight.

Or consider this example. Mr. Smith was for years the "glue" that held Piney Grove church together. When Mr. Smith died there was no one available to take his place, to do as well as he did the "gluing" of that congregation. The congregation became a splintered, disparate collection of factions that wandered now here, now there, without any sense of cohesiveness.

Birth can have just as profound an impact as death. At First Church the small group of young couples began to start families. The church began to think through in ways it had not considered for twenty years the possible need for a nursery in the church, a new young couples' class, and a preschool program that might require placing some of the best teachers in the church school in the preschool division. And the church had to consider whether to include these young couples in its leadership. Some people are born and some people die. That is a major internal source of change.

A second internal source of change is the coming and leaving of people. In a given church the central leader of the music program was transferred by her employer to another community. A year later people were discussing the fact that their pastor's preaching was not what it used to be. Upon closer examination it was discovered that before the music leader had been transferred, she as choir director had been delivering a choir of thirty highly motivated, enthusiastic persons each Sunday. The music was most dynamic and inspiring. When she was transferred the church leaders did the best they could to replace her as choir director. The new choir director was an excellent person, young—in her early twenties—and doing the best she could. And when I heard the phrase "doing the best she could," I knew what had happened; the total impact of the service was not as dynamic and inspiring as it had been. The choir was down to seventeen members. But church members felt that surely it could not be the homegrown choir director, "doing the best she could," who was responsible for the lack of dynamism. It really must be that the preaching was not as strong as it was before.

The converse is equally the case. I have been in churches across the land where the coming of new people with rich new gifts and competencies has substantially helped to grow forward a given congregation. To be sure, in some communities one is considered a newcomer until he or she has lived there for eighteen years. And at the same time some people who come to a church have excellent skills in getting on board as they move into the new community. Equally important, some of the people who come are not really newcomers. I can remember the Sunday when Bill came first to church. He was the chief of the volunteer fire department in the community. He was an excellent person, and he was also known to have his fair share of problems with drinking. That Sunday as he walked in there was a hush. Reluctantly at first, and then fully and richly, that congregation accepted Bill. The congregation was never the same from that day forward because of the arrival of that person.

I remember helping a church in the mountains of north Georgia. In the choir that Sunday morning was a sixteen-year-old girl who was clearly very pregnant under her choir robe. She had come, pregnant and unmarried. Her family had turned her out. She lived now here, now there, in the early months of her pregnancy. Then one Sunday morning, halfway through her pregnancy, she came to that church. And in amazing ways that church took her in. Now think of the pilgrimage that congregation went through when they took her in, overcoming all sorts of injunctions about never being pregnant outside of wedlock, let alone at sixteen, let alone without the support of one's family. With the arrival of that person the church became richly and fully a changed congregation.

The third source of internal change is that some people grow and develop and some people do not. As people grow and develop in their own life's pilgrimage, their contributions, their perspective, and their perceptions related to their own congregation grow and develop as well. To be sure, John was an excellent auto mechanic; he liked to do things with his hands and was extraordinarily good with tools. And John was profoundly puzzled as to the meaning and purpose of everyday, ordinary life in the light of the gospel. It was out of his searchings, discussions, readings, and reflections that John's own sense of life's meaning and purpose grew and developed. As that growth and development took place John's contributions to his church substantially changed. Many people in that church began to discover new ways in which life has value, meaning, and purpose in the light of the gospel.

Some people grow and develop in this life's pilgrimage and their contributions decisively affect the local church. I invite you to be thinking of the several events of internal change that are distinctive and decisive for your church. As leaders, think through the ways in which internal sources of change have contributed to where your congregation now is and where it is likely to be in the days and years to come.

Conflict

The third dynamic that has decisive impact in local churches is the dynamic of conflict. There are three sources of conflict in a congregation. The first is what I call the "best of families" conflict. Even in the best of families there is a fair share of conflict. Even between people who deeply love one another and have lived together as husband and wife for thirty or more years, there will occasionally be a conflict. Sometimes two sisters don't speak to one another for a period of time. Sometimes one brother has a tendency to beat up another brother. Sometimes a husband and wife have been known to shout at each other. Sometimes one brother will be at his father's house, taking the mementos that he just knows his father would want him to have, even as the other brother is at the funeral home making the arrangements for their father's funeral. There is a considerable share of conflict and strife in the best of families.

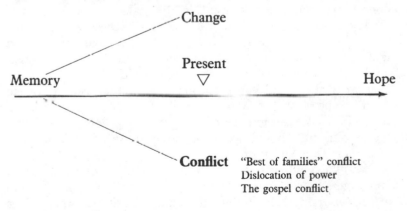

Figure 11.   The Dynamic of Conflict

What distinguishes the best of families is their capacity for forgiveness, reconciliation, and moving on, not the absence of conflict. The only people I know who don't have conflict are the people buried in the nearest cemetery. And sometimes I'm not so sure about them—when I walk by late at night, I hear murmurings and mutterings. Conflict is present in the best of families.

We sometimes think that the best we can do is model ourselves after the early church. Read freshly Paul's letter to the church at Galatia, which had its raging conflicts. What marks the best of churches is the congregation's capacity for forgiveness, reconciliation, and moving on, not the absence of conflict.

The second source of conflict is the trend in our country toward dislocation of power. Over the past forty years power has been dislocated from local and regional sources to national and international sources. As a result people in our time have experienced a pervasive sense of powerlessness. For many, many people the decisions that affect their lives and shape their destinies are made somewhere else by someone else, and one can't quite always find out who or what or where.

You go down to the courthouse to transact a simple bit of business and go to the new courthouse annex. You are directed up to the second floor, third door on the right. You visit with a pleasant gray-haired lady who tells you that that used to be done there, but it is now done in the state capital. You write the state capital and you get a letter back that says that it used to be done there, but it is now done in a regional office. You write the regional office and you get a letter back that says it used to be done there, but it is now done in Washington, D.C. You write them and you get a letter back that says if you go down to the new courthouse annex, second floor, third door on the right, a pleasant gray-haired lady will help you. Lots of people in our time experience a profound sense of powerlessness over their lives and destinies.

The two symptoms of this sense of powerlessness are apathy and anger. I am frequently invited as church consultant to help a local church think through the apathy of its members. It is not as simple as church apathy. If one looks closely at those persons who are expressing apathy, one discovers that in all spheres and sectors of their lives—the religious, social, civic, communal, vocational, educational, economic, recreational, familial, and political arenas—there is a sense of apathy. And it is not as simple as saying, "If people only had more commitment, they wouldn't be apathetic." The truth of the matter is, if people had more power—if people had the sense that they had more power over their own lives and destinies—then, to be sure, they would express less apathy.

The second clue to this pervasive sense of powerlessness is anger. Frequently people bring their anger with them to our churches. They displace their anger in church—where else can they share their anger? Indeed, they have some hopes that surely in the church people will understand the profound roots of their anger and accept, love, and care for them, even as they express that anger. Sometimes in a board meeting people vent anger over the most trivial thing and others do not always understand what is happening. Frequently what is happening is that those people are displacing anger from some other sector of their lives in the one place they hope people will understand and accept them, namely, their church. It is a whole lot safer to shout one's anger over apportionments than it is to shout one's anger over the actions of the Internal Revenue Service.

Sometimes people are rightfully angry in a church because that church has lost its focus on people, service, and mission and has become too preoccupied with money, maintenance, and membership issues. People have a genuine right to be angry when a church loses its way in this fashion. At the same time it is important to understand that displaced anger is a clue to the pervasive sense of powerlessness many people feel in our culture.

Some church historians suggest that in the eighteenth century John Wesley saved England from the bloodbaths that were occurring across the channel during the French Revolution. And that the way in which Wesley saved England from those bloodbaths was through the class meetings, where people who had experienced a profound sense of powerlessness discovered constructive, creative ways to recover power for the shaping of their own lives and destinies.

The third source of conflict is the gospel. Now, it is *not* true that whenever there is conflict one can automatically assume that the gospel is being shared. Some pastors make the foolish mistake of assuming that simply because they are involved in conflict they are involved in sharing the gospel. They may, in fact, be involved in a "best of families" kind of conflict, or they may be involved in a dislocation-of-power kind of conflict. Just because it is conflict does not mean that the gospel is being shared.

Some churches assume that because they are stable and declining they are therefore in mission. The truth of the matter is that they are not delivering nine out of the twelve central characteristics, and that is why they are stable and declining—they may or may not be in mission. Some pastors assume that when they are losing members it is a sign they are preaching the gospel. Sometimes this is the case, and sometimes it is simply the case that this church is not delivering nine out of the twelve central characteristics or that the pastor's preaching is inept or both.

At the same time it is a fact of life that the gospel nurtures conflict. That certainly is a part of the biblical message. Whenever we are invited to leave off old ways and come to new ways in Christ, there will be a fair share of tension and conflict as we sort through whether the values of this world and culture are the values with which we want to live through this life's pilgrimage. Wherever the gospel is richly and fully preached, people will struggle with the conflict of decision as to the direction of their life and destiny. That tension, that conflict, that decisive calling to a new way is important, and it is important that such a spirit of conflict be amply and fully present in a local church, or that church is no longer a church.

As leaders, look for and discern the sources of conflict in your congregation. I invite you to be thinking of the several events of conflict that are distinctive and decisive for your church. What range of conflicts are expressions of "best of families" conflicts? What range of conflicts are expressions of dislocations of power? What range of conflicts are appropriately and importantly expressions of the gospel's calling to new life? As leaders, you will want to be sensitive to the ways in which the dynamic of conflict affects the present life of your congregation and its future.

Hope

Of the four dynamics the strongest is hope. People live on hope, not on memory. Take away people's memories and they become anxious. Take away people's hopes and they become terrified. People long for and look for some sense of hope, some understanding of a reliable and certain future.

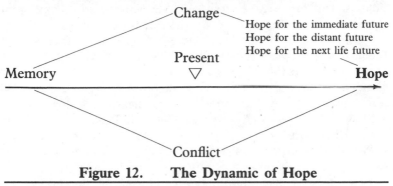

Figure 12.   The Dynamic of Hope

People look for hope in the immediate future. If they cannot see some sources of hope in the immediate future, they then look for hope in the distant future. And if they cannot see some sources of hope in the distant future, they then look for some sources of hope in the next life future. People postpone their hopes down the road. If they cannot see some immediate fulfillment in either the immediate or the distant future, they will long for and look for some of their deepest hopes, yearnings, and longings to be fulfilled in the next life's future.

Some key leaders and pastors make the mistake of assuming that the art of developing an effective long-range plan is to drag people reluctantly from the customs, habits, and traditions of the past into the present and the immediate future. What pastors and key leaders frequently miss is that many people are not living in the past—they are living in the next life future. Many people in our culture have postponed their hopes to the next life—they can see no way in which their hopes, even some of them, will be reasonably fulfilled in the immediate future or the distant future. And so they are living in the next life future.

A sociologist once did a study in Appalachia and concluded that the pioneers who cut down trees and built log cabins in those early years had moved into Appalachia with a confident vision of hope and that they saw themselves engaged in the building of a new and promised land. But the sociologist concluded that those persons who now live in Appalachia eke out a bare, meager existence, clinging and clutching desperately to life, and no longer share their ancestors' sense of confident hope in the building of a new promised land. The one place the sociologist had failed to go was to those white-frame, clapboard churches up the hollows and on the ridges on Sunday morning and listen to the hymns sung there—"We Shall Gather at the River," "In the Sweet By-and-By," "Dwelling in Beulah Land." People postpone their hopes. When people cannot see the fulfillment of some of their hopes in the immediate or distant future, they postpone their hopes to their next life future.

I have good friends all across the South and some of my black friends there used to sing the song, "We Shall Overcome," in a "Sweet By-and-By" way. And then they began to sing that song in marching ways, counting on and looking forward to some of their deepest hopes being fulfilled in the immediate future, not just in the next life's future. And one clear source of resentment between some of my white, sharecropping friends and some of my black friends in the South is as follows: If white sharecroppers can see no fulfillment of some of their hopes in the immediate and distant future, how can a black have the audacity to assume that some of his or her hopes will be fulfilled in the immediate or distant future?

People live on hope, not on memory. At Bethlehem Church on a Sunday morning, Mrs. Lott and I were standing out on the front porch of the church. Most of the people had gone, and it hadn't taken that long because there weren't that many people to have gone. She said to me, "Ken, what I hope is that you will send to us a preacher this coming year that will share with us spiritual food." What she was saying was that her husband had retired from the farm and was ambling about the house with little to do, and her mother was ill and dying in a nearby nursing home. And there were now strange, new kinds of people living up and down Flowery Springs Road who stayed up past ten o'clock at night and dressed differently, and one or two of them had motorcycles. What she was saying was that the hopeful ways in which she had made sense of life for the past twenty to twenty-five years were no longer working for her as well, and she wanted a pastor who would help her to make some sense out of everyday life with a degree of hope that would be realized in the present and the immediate future, not simply the next life future.

At New Liberty Church, when the kids rode their horses across the church cemetery, people got upset. People got upset not simply because they thought the horses and the kids were desecrating the ancestors of the past but because the horses and the kids were trampling on that church's symbol of the future. That church cemetery is not primarily a symbol of the past. The people know that those who are buried there are not really there. They only fix the cemetery up once a year, just before homecoming. They want to be buried there not so they can lie beside so and so, but because that cemetery is the symbol of each family's entrance into the kingdom of hope beyond this life. To be sure, the cemetery honors those who have gone before. But most important, the focus is on where they have gone—to a new and promised land, the land of hope. People want to be buried there because that cemetery is equally and fully the symbol of the future.

Many, many churches across our country have a homecoming each year. Church homecomings are not events that look to the past only. Church homecomings are events that look to the future. The homecoming is a present day, proleptic event that looks to that great homecoming "beyond the river" when all will be gathered as God's family.

One reason many persons find themselves drawn to churches that preach quaint, nonsensical, foolish apocalyptic understandings of the future is because those persons are desperately searching for some sense of hope. However quaint, nonsensical, foolish, and apocalyptic the promise of hope in that church, at least it has the echo of hope about it. Too many of our churches have services of worship that conclude on the cross. Too many of our churches have services of worship that include sermons with a fifteen- to eighteen-minute problem analysis and a quick, closing generality that "Jesus is the answer." Most people know their problems reasonably well. What people come to a church longing and looking for is a sense of help, a sense of home, and a sense of hope. And people are even drawn to those churches that can only promise a tawdry sense of hope.

Nostalgia is not a retreat to the past. Nostalgia is looking back to a time when some of our deepest hopes and longings were fulfilled and drawing that picture forward as the only picture of the future to which we can cling, because no clearer picture seems available to us. We are all wise enough to know that Grover's Corners is no more. To be sure, it may exist now here, now there, in some hidden valley not yet discovered in the last half of the twentieth century. But the "Our Towns" of our planet, like the town in Thornton Wilder's play *Our Town*, are no more. There everybody went to bed at ten o'clock at night, and the train went through about the same time every night. There Emily and George married. But even in Grover's Corners, Emily died in childbirth. Grover's Corners is no more. Nostalgia is an effort to put before us some picture of hope when no other picture of hope seems possible.

I have helped many churches that were frozen on the face of a cliff. Think about mountain climbing. Think about what it is like to find oneself on the face of a cliff where one cannot reach the handholds and footholds behind or ahead. What does a person do in that predicament? That person does one thing extraordinarily well. He or she freezes to the face of the cliff and clutches and clings for dear life.

Some churches are like that. They can find no handholds and footholds of the past to go back to, and they can find no handholds and footholds for the future. They cling and clutch for dear life to the face of the cliff and freeze, immobile, desiring no change.

And, to be sure, you and I, frozen to the face of the cliff, would not want very much change either. And then some cheery person comes along at the top of the cliff and hollers down in a loud voice, "Oh, it's simple! Just do as I tell you." You and I know what happens next. The person frozen to the face of the cliff is disrupted, alarmed even more. The person loses his or her handholds and falls into the abyss below.

What one does with a person frozen to the face of a cliff is gently and quietly coach them. Here is this handhold. Here is this foothold. Now here is another handhold. Now here is this foothold. And sometimes, gently and quietly, inch by inch, it is possible to coach the person forward to new handholds and footholds. The same is true of churches. Good key leaders gently and quietly coach their churches forward to new handholds and new footholds.

Two things are true about the kingdom: The kingdom has come, and the kingdom is coming. The reality of the kingdom has happened, and its fulfillment is before us.

The kingdom is now here, now there. That is, the kingdom "happens" in every event of reconciliation, wholeness, caring, and justice. These events are proleptic experiences of the kingdom. Where Christ is, there is the kingdom.

At the same time, the kingdom is not yet—in its fullness. Some people share only half of the good news. Some people speak only of the this-worldly kingdom. Others focus only on an other-worldly, next-life understanding of the kingdom. Both groups are wrong. The truth of the kingdom is twofold: the kingdom is now here, now there, *and* the kingdom is not yet in its fullness.

What is needed in many of our churches is a profound, rich, full theology of hope. There is direct correlation between effective long-range planning and eschatology—theology of hope, theology of the future. The two go hand in hand. One cannot do one without the other. It is only in a theology strongly influenced by eschatology that a dynamic understanding of the future—that is, mission by objectives—could have been developed.

Many of the mainline denominations in our country have virtually no rich, full eschatology. They have given that field over to sectarian, quaint apocalyptic understandings of eschatology that are nonsensical and foolish. And when denominations abandon a rich, full eschatology, they are then in a weaker position to do effective long-range planning. Eschatology informs effective long-range planning, and effective long-range planning informs eschatology. The two go hand in hand. What we need in our time is the development of a richer, fuller, more profound theology of hope and of the future that takes seriously the dynamics of conflict, change, and memory.

As leaders, it is helpful for you to think through the dynamic of hope as it currently expresses itself in your congregation and to grow forward a rich, full, profound theology of hope as you do effective long-range planning. I invite you to be thinking of the several events of hope that are distinctive and decisive for your church, that affect the present and future of a congregation.

Of the four dynamics that affect the present and future of a congregation—memory, change, conflict, and hope—the strongest is hope.

Conclusion: Mission and Compassion

God calls the church to be *in* the center of people's lives, not to *be* the center of their lives. God has richly blessed us. We live on one of the richest mission fields on the planet. And God calls us to a new day. We no longer live in the churched culture of the 1950s, if indeed it ever existed. The day of the busy, bustling post–World War II suburban church as the center of people's lives is over. The day of the mission congregation *in* the center of people's lives has come.

In this new day effective long-range plans do not look like those of an extinct churched culture. They look like the long-range plans of a people on a mission field; they focus on mission and compassion, service, and the world.

In this new day effective long-range plans focus more on mission and compassion than on membership and maintenance. The purpose of planning in this new day is not to press people to spend more time at church but to help people invest the gifts and competencies, which they have received from God, in the world.

Those churches that continue to behave as though this were still the churched culture of the 1950s do one thing very well. They successfully become stable and declining or dying churches. A pastor or key leader who still behaves as though it were the post–World War II churched culture of the 1950s can be compared to the captain on the bridge of a disabled ship. He or she presides with honor and dignity as the ship slowly founders and sinks into the depths of the sea beneath.

So long as the church seeks to be the center of people's lives, it is no different from the other entities of our culture that clamor to gain the central place in people's lives. When the church decides to be in the center of people's lives, the church transcends the entities of the culture; it gives up its own self-seeking, survival-oriented tendencies and becomes an entity focused on compassion, on serving, sharing, and caring. Whenever the church does this the church is truly the church.

In an earlier time it may have been possible to get away with developing long-range plans that focused on membership and maintenance. No more. The day of mission and compassion has come. The day of membership and maintenance is over.

Service

Whether a given local church survives or not is in God's hands. Some of our local churches will one day be footnotes in dusty books on church history. Be at peace about that. We are called not to endure but to serve. God calls us to focus on service, not survival. God calls us to be in the center of people's lives, serving human hurts and hopes. God calls us to a mission of reconciliation, wholeness, caring, and justice. God calls us not to seek survival but to share service.

One can read a church bulletin or a church newsletter and sense whether that local church is committed to service or preoccupied with survival. One can listen to a sermon and sense where that pastor's concern is. One can sit in a meeting and sense the preoccupation of that church. In some meetings it is a regular practice to share information on who has moved and who has died this past month. Hardly ever is it a regular practice to share information on who has been helped in mission this past month or who has discovered Christ this past month.

If you want to worry, worry about something that counts. To worry about whether your local church will survive is to worry about a lesser thing. To worry for the human hurts and hopes of the many people who have yet to discover Christ—now that is a worry that counts!

We spend too much time trying to get people to come to the church building. We need to invest more time being the church with the people in the world. How many times have you heard it said (and with pride), "We were there every time the church doors were open?" I would guess you have heard it far more often than, "We were there to help when a person experienced hurt and hope." The locus of the church in a churched culture is the church building. The locus of the church on a mission field is at the front lines of human hurts and hopes.

There is an ancient document, now and then found at hotels and motels. On rare occasions someone opens the long-lost manuscript and discovers these quietly powerful words: "For whoever would save his life will lose it, and whoever loses his life for my sake will find it" (Matt. 16:25 RSV).

This applies to local churches as well as to individuals. Apply this passage from Matthew to your local church. "If any local church would come after me, let that local church deny itself and take up its cross and follow me. For whatever church would save its life will lose it, and whatever church loses its life for my sake will find it. For what will it profit a local church if it gains the world [by comparison, two hundred new members seems small] and forfeits its life [its primary reason to exist, its true mission]?" (Matt. 16:24–26 RSV paraphrased).

The World

A few pastors and key leaders still behave as though Copernicus had never lived. Copernicus helped us to see that the earth is not the center of the world—the sun is the center of this solar system. Likewise the church building is not the center of the mission. The world is the center of the mission. Just because a few people and a few pastors have decided to make the church building the center of their lives does not mean that everyone should. Indeed, in this new day some pastors and key leaders will want to rethink God's calling for them—was it to the church building or to mission? A few pastors think their place of work is their office. Not so. Their place of work is in the world.

A pastor, recently graduated from seminary, took up his post at his first church. Upon arrival his first two questions were, "Where is my office?" and "When is my first meeting?" These two questions are archeological relics left over from the churched culture of the 1950s. In this new day the best first two questions are, "Where is our mission?" and "Where are our people?"

It is understandable that a few pastors and key leaders would want the church to be the center of every person's life. These people have decided to make the church the center of their lives. Therefore, it is natural that they would want others to share the same commitment. But the premise is the problem. Pastors are not called to make the church the center of their lives. Pastors are called to make God's mission the center of their lives.

We have come to a time when many pastors know they have been called to serve a mission field—a whole community—not solely a local church. We have come to a time when many local churches know their task is to serve people in the community, not to have people in the community serve that church.

The focus of the church is not the church building. The focus of the church is the world. God is in the world. Whenever the church is *in* the world, God is in the church. Whenever the church is not in the world, God is not in the church. God does not forsake the world for the church. God is still in the world. In John 3:16 we discover these words: "For God so loved the world [the word is not *church*] that he gave his only Son . . ." (RSV). God calls the church to be *in* the center of people's lives, not to be the center of their lives.

God has planted us on one of the richest mission fields on the planet. Just when some of us had begun to think life was almost over and we simply had to stay out of too much trouble until the end, God has given us a new day. God calls us to rethink the center and focus of our work.

Your Long-range Plan

As you decide your long-range plan you are deciding how your life will count. Most persons want their lives to count. Your life will count more as you invest it in mission and compassion.

On a mission field many key leaders of churches invest their time in the world more than in the church. Some may protest tentatively that this is too idealistic. Not so. Whoever would suggest that is the idealist, still living in the churched culture of the 1950s. I am being the realist, not the idealist. We live on a mission field. And an effective long-range plan takes that realistically and seriously.

Use well the principles and resources in the *Leaders' Guide*. Use well the *Planning Workbook* and *Twelve Keys to an Effective Church*. Discover, develop, and decide the long-range plan that matches best with your current strengths and the community—the mission field—your church seeks to serve. Build a strong dynamic of action, implementation, and momentum.

My hope is that your long-range plan will not generate more programs and activities, more meetings and maintenance, more committees and agencies. Rather, my hope is that your long-range plan will generate the following:

- Mission teams, the likes of which your community and the world have not yet seen
- Visitation and shepherding teams that deliver sharing and caring with persons served in mission, constituents, and members
- Worship and prayer teams that give the world, your community, and your church a new vision of hope
- Leaders who start an ever increasing number of significant relational groups—to deliver roots, place, and belonging—amidst the societal dislocation and psychological disorientation of our times.

We have loved our local churches too much. They will come and go, rise and fall, grow and die. What endures is the mission of God. God calls your church to mission. God calls your church not to *be* the center of people's lives, but rather to be *in* the center of their lives. May God give you compassion and peace, wisdom and judgment, vision and common sense. My prayer is that the mission of God be with you in the days to come.

Hope is stronger than memory. Salvation is stronger than sin. Forgiveness is stronger than bitterness. Reconciliation is stronger than hatred. Light is stronger than darkness. Resurrection is stronger than crucifixion. The open tomb is stronger than the bloodied cross. The risen Lord is stronger than the dead Jesus. Easter is stronger than Good Friday. Hope is stronger than memory.

We are the Easter people. We are the people of hope. We are the people of the open tomb, the risen Lord, and new life in Christ.